She Speaks to Me

{ WESTERN WOMEN'S VIEW OF THE WEST THROUGH POETRY AND SONG }

Jill Charlotte Stanford

WITH PHOTOGRAPHS BY ROBIN L. GREEN

TWODOT®

GUILFORD, CONNECTICUT
HELENA, MONTANA

A · TWODOT® · BOOK

An imprint and registered trademark of Rowman & Littlefield

Distributed by NATIONAL BOOK NETWORK

British Library Cataloguing-in-Publication Information available

Library of Congress Cataloging-in-Publication Data available

ISBN 978-1-4930-1903-8 (paperback)
ISBN 978-1-4930-1904-5 (e-book)

♾™ The paper used in this publication meets the minimum requirements of American National Standard for Information Sciences—Permanence of Paper for Printed Library Materials, ANSI/ NISO Z39.48-1992.

With respect and loving gratitude for her
enthusiastic help and wise encouragement,
this book is dedicated to Virginia Bennett

CONTENTS

FOREWORD

For centuries different cultures have relied on songs and stories for entertainment and to pass down history and traditions. In the mid-1800s, during the epic cattle drives through the wide open spaces of the American West, cowboys occupied long, lonely hours in the saddle and nights watching cattle or sitting by the campfire by composing stories to share. Some of these tales were shaped in verse or lyrical form, with rhyme and meter that made them easy to remember so they could be retold and even put to a galloping melody.

The cowboys were primarily former Civil War soldiers and emigrants. Though the poems and songs were often bleak and starkly realistic, conveying the perils and hardships of the cowboys' work, they often contained colorful words from different languages that had worked their way into contemporary cowboy lingo. The lyrics were set to old folk ballads from the Old World. They told of harsh weather conditions, lonesomeness, wild broncs, and stampedes. They were written by cowboys for cowboys, and in their own language. By the turn of the late 1800s and early 1900s, cowboy poetry and Western music had become oral traditions and viable genres in print and recording.

As fences created a checkerboard on the range and large, privately owned ranches were established, cowboy poetry made its way into livestock journals and published collections of poetry, and the themes changed to fit a new age of the cattle industry. The poems left much to the imagination of readers, and soon the Western lifestyle was being romanticized by Hollywood actors in film and on radio broadcasts. Dashingly handsome and witty, riding a polished horse with silver-adorned saddle, the cowboy developed a heroic image that personified the freedom and spirit of the West. It was not an authentic portrayal of the original cowboys, who were considered poor, uneducated, second-class citizens. Silver screen cowboys usually had a sidekick and, in the case of Roy Rogers, it was his equally idyllic cowgirl, Dale Evans.

Though women played a role in settling and shaping the image of the West, their primary role was seen as fulfilling domestic duties such as birthing and raising children, tending the home, and stitching a family together. The writings of early Western women were omitted from traditional cowboy collections, though they were just as valid and authentic.

The rise of organized cowboy poetry gatherings, starting in the 1980s, gave the voices of Western women a place to be heard. Today, women play a significant role in chronicling the contemporary West through poetry and song, enriching cowboy culture with their feminine perspectives on such topics as faith, family, horses, cowboys, cattle, and the land. Using these vehicles as their springboards, their work evokes sensitivity and sentimentality, yet inspires readers with the same grit, tenacity, and independent spirit that has made cowboy poetry so popular.

She Speaks to Me: Western Women's View of the West Through Poetry and Song is an anthology of poetry and song lyrics written by contemporary women who not only appreciate ranch life and the West, but also live and breathe it in their daily lives. Many women are doing the work of men on family ranches. There is no "he or she" or "his or her work." It is all work that needs to be done by whomever can do it, and the men depend greatly on the wives/mothers/sisters/daughters in the family. These salt-of-the-earth women have earned every scar, wrinkle, callus, and laugh line on their skin, and have stories to go with them. They are all dedicated to riding for the brand. They know how to stretch a dollar, cook a meal of comfort food that fills up a large crew, patch well-worn shirts and jeans, heal a scrape with a kiss, and juggle responsibilities to which women of all walks of life can relate. In between, they find quiet moments to observe and appreciate the simple things, like the colors of a sunrise or the sound of jingling spurs and horses hooves, and to find humor in mundane chores like doing laundry and milking cows, and many of them write it down in the form of a poem or a song lyric.

Editor Jill Charlotte Stanford shares the cowgirl spirit of these women, and a special kinship with them that gave her a rare ability to round up thirty of the best poets and singer-songwriters and compile their most poignant works into a lively volume that will leave readers laughing, wiping tears, shaking their heads in amazement, and sometimes nodding in agreement. Short biographies on each wordsmith, complemented by dynamic photographs by Robin L. Green, offer insight into the lives and personalities of each woman.

—Jennifer Denison, senior editor,
Western Horseman

PROLOGUE

"The true poem rests between the words."

—Author unknown

The first poetry written and recited by a cowgirl I ever heard was in Burns, Oregon, in 2010. The poet was Jessica Hedges. She stood up in front of the audience—many of them ranchers and their families—wearing her trademark "flat hat" of a buckaroo, boots, and jeans. She began reciting a poem she had written about waiting for her buckaroo husband to return home. He had ridden out to check on some pregnant cows. It was getting late and getting dark. She was worried. She was waiting to hear the bell on his cinch, signaling his return. As she spoke, I could feel her fear, hear her concern out there on the high desert, alone in the house save for a sleeping baby boy, and miles from the nearest neighbor. I was hardly aware that she was speaking in rhyme. Her hands described things in the air. Often, she would pause and listen for that bell. Heck, we were *all* listening for that bell, which she finally heard. It ended well: Her buckaroo was home safe. But, for a moment . . . I was there with her, in that room, listening, worried . . .

It takes a certain amount of courage, grit, and gumption to not only compose a poem, but also to write it down, and then to stand up in front of total strangers and recite what, until that moment, had been your own personal view of your life and the hardships, joys, and triumphs it holds. The poetry written by the women of the West, who spend their days on horseback or on a tractor, tending children, riding herd on cattle, helping with the harvest, enduring bone-chilling cold and searing summer heat, raising an orphan calf, foal, lamb, or puppy in the kitchen, doctoring sick or injured animals (and that includes the humans too), cooking three meals a day, often out in the middle of nowhere in a house that loses its tentative connection to electricity and the outside world fairly often, offers a special glimpse into the lives that inspire that grit and gumption, and the moments of uncertainty that punctuate them.

That night in Burns, another young cowgirl recited a poem she had written about life with her family, dogs, horses, and cattle on a ranch outside of town. Randi Johnson spoke with humor and insight, and again, I was transfixed by the trueness of the words I was hearing. It was like music, carrying us along with cadence and meter, punctuated now and then by a line that made the audience chuckle. They knew what she was talking about. Her poetry reached them. It was true. She "spoke" to them. I never forgot that evening.

Not long after, I was poking around in a used bookstore and came across a small volume titled *Voices from the Range* by Rhoda Sivell. A picture of a bucking bronco with a cowboy losing his hat but "sticking with it" got my money out of my wallet, and I took the book home. It is a charming collection of the author's "cowboy" poetry, published in Toronto, Canada, in 1912. Rhoda Cosgrave Sivell (1874-1962) was an Irish émigré who, with her husband, ranched near Medicine Hat, Alberta.

Just imagine what life out on the Canadian prairie was like! Cold in the winter, winds that never stopped howling around the cabin, no near neighbors, and always, the day-to-day work of ranching. The fact that Rhoda found the time to sit down with a pencil and paper, with only an oil lamp to see by, and write her poems makes this collection very precious to me.

The opening lines of her poem "The Hard Winter" speaks volumes:

> We knew we were up against it,
> For the snow on the hills lay deep:
> It drifted into the coulees,
> And most of the drifts ten feet.
> *(Ten feet!)*

Say that stanza aloud and you will "hear" a true poet, a woman who put into words what life out there on the bleak landscape was like in the depths of winter.

For me, one discovery like this seemed to lead to another, and I was entranced by the variety of voices I came across, especially when I asked other cowgirls and Western women around me who their favorite poets were. Caprice Madison, a cowgirl who spends the summer/fall season working for an outfitter in the wilderness of Colorado with her husband, Sam, himself a bronc rider, shared her favorite with me. The legendary cowgirl/outlaw Belle Starr is credited with having written this poem:

Bucking Bronco

My love is a rider, wild broncos he breaks,
Though he's promised to quit it, just for my sake.
He ties up one foot, the saddle puts on,
With a swing and a jump he is mounted and gone.
The first time I met him, 'twas early one spring,
Riding a Bronco, a high-headed thing.
He tipped me a wink as he gaily did go,
For he wished me to look at his Bucking Bronco.
The next time I saw him, 'twas late in the fall,
Swinging the girls at the Tomlinson's ball:
He laughed and he talked as we danced to and fro,
Promised never to ride on another bronco.
He made me presents, among them a ring;
The return that I made him was a far better thing;
'Twas a young maiden's heart, I'd have you all know
He'd won it by riding his Bucking Bronco.
Now all you young maidens, where'er you reside,
Beware of the cowboy who swings the rawhide,
He'll court you and pet you and leave you and go
In the spring up the trail on his Bucking Bronco.

I asked more of my cowgirl and ranching friends to tell me who their favorite cowgirl poet or songwriter was—whose poetry "speaks to them" while they are out on the John Deere, or on horseback, or stirring a pot of stew at the stove. Every one of them had a favorite. The poets, like the listeners and readers, live the same life and share the same passion for the West.

In this collection are the poems of cowgirl poets who are regulars at the numerous state, local, and national cowboy poetry gatherings that happen throughout the year. There are a few songwriters as well—after all, their songs are simply poetry set to music. Some of the poets have never been published and were shy about being included, but the true poet is always, just under the surface, eager to have her voice heard. Why else would she go to the trouble? The poets and songwriters featured here were quick to respond to the invitation to be included. In true Western fashion, they saddled their fast ponies and galloped in with their poetry and lyrics for your enjoyment.

Gifted photographer Robin L. Green chose the captivating photographs to accompany these lovely verses and songs. She captures the stark, lush, brutal, gentle, and ever-changing Western landscape and the creatures that inhabit it (including intrepid humans) in all sorts of weather—harsh or gentle—like no other.

Virginia Bennett, a noted poet and to whom this book is dedicated, wrote to me, "So, I'm imagining readers come in all shapes and sizes and you are corralling all shapes and sizes of poetry, not 'one size fits all.' I think that should be met with positive reactions, don't you?" I certainly hope so, Virginia! Virginia and numerous other cowgirls pointed me in the direction of their favorite poets, and some of those cowgirls' words are featured here, as well.

This book has been, for me, something of a gift. Not only was I blessed to read and "hear" this wonderfully crafted verse about a place and a lifestyle I cherish—the West—but I also made the acquaintance of the talented, generous, and giving women who wrote the words you are about to experience. Many of them I count as good friends now. I am completely in awe of them.

So, "sit back, drop the reins," as Joni Harms writes, and "listen" to the words of the *true* Western experience.

—Jill Charlotte Stanford

She Speaks to Me

AMY HALE AUKER

Prescott, Arizona

Amy Hale Auker cowboys on a ranch in the Santa Maria Mountains of Arizona with her husband, Gail Steiger. I know she carries a small notebook in the pocket of her work shirt so she can catch the moments as they fly by.

Amy is the author of *Rightful Place*, the 2012 WILLA winner for creative nonfiction, as well as two novels, *Winter of Beauty* and *The Story Is the Thing*. She likes to guide her readers to, as she puts it, "a place where the bats fly, lizards do push-ups on the rocks, and bears leave barefoot prints in the dirt. Where hummingbirds do rain dances in August, spiders weave for their food, and poetry is in the chrysalis and the cocoon." Amy tells stories about the real world where things grow up out of the ground, where the miracle of life happens over and over and over again, where people can—and do—survive without malls or Arby's.

Teach Me to See

Born blind,
and didn't even know it.
Thought I could, thought I was,
missed not only the minutiae
but the broad vistas.
I missed the unveiling, the lifting of scales.
I am learning, but slowly.
Teach me to see.

Teach me to see that
In the chrysalis, the caterpillar.
In the nymph, the dragonfly.
At the edge of the web, the spider.
Dark sky wings transition at dusk
when the swallow becomes the bat.
Painted canvas hills cradle
creeks, clear with amoeba and skaters.
I see the pinch bug carrying her eggs
until the waterfall wins without trying.
I see the shed skin of a snake
lining the nest of a bird,
lifted from ground, introduced to sky.

Teach me to see
Beyond my nation,
Beyond my appetite.
More than tracks in the dust,
to see the barefoot bear foot.
To see past the words
or agendas
or ones and zeros
or ancient Jungian bleed.

I see the shadow of his daddy's hands
in his newborn fist.
I see the bruised eyes of love
wrecked on the reef of self,
the closed criticized child,
the laundry list of needing more,
the confusion of colossal change.

Amongst the boulders and the trees
I begin to see.
Simply. And that is to be.
Teach me to see.

Things Worth Writing a Poem About

It's the cowboy riding two hours
to the top of Elbow Spring,
for that last little group of cows,
but turning, he rides home again,
leaving them behind,
while in juniper shade
the goat-horned heifer
licks her first calf.
He'll come back when the time is right.

It's yellow toadstools two days after the rain,
and rock echeveria when it blooms.

It's this phone call:
Mr. Clark? It's Travis.
About tomorrow . . .
Oh, she's fine. Biggr'n a house, but we have two weeks yet.
No, sir, I don't need to stay home,
it's just that when I went to hook up my trailer tonight,
well, see, there's a bird nest in the nose,
and I'd just pull it out, but the eggs have already hatched,
and well, I was just wondering,
could I maybe borrow a horse?

It's riding so long
you aren't hungry anymore,
hearing a zone tail above the branding pen,
a fox's mating call at dawn,
a bull screaming for girls in the night.

Amy Hale Auker

3

It's the boss who hangs up the phone,
smiling,
knowing he made the right choice
when he hired that kid.

It's my Papa,
at ninety,
holding a great-grandson on his knee,
after bath time,
running life-scarred hands over
tender toddler skin,
looking up at his granddaughter to say,
"My, he has good hide."

It's knowing
where the bull snake lives
and that the cows know better than I do how to get down off this slope.

It's knowing that the bat has sex in the fall,
but doesn't get pregnant 'til spring,
when the time is right.

His Time of Day

The old cow moves and stretches her bones
from her place in the cedar shade.
She calls to her calf, drawing him close,
teaching him to not be afraid.

The man and his horse have just arrived
with his smells and his sounds, his woo.
She sniffs the wind for the hint of hay.
He is making a pasture move.

The red cow turns, walks up the dim trail
with four more of her closest friends.
Their calves are all about the same age
and possibly distantly kin.

Years past her ears would have dripped with dogs
and his horse would have foamed with sweat.
Today they walk in a quiet line,
to join more on the salt ground, he bets.

He values now drives gentle and slow.
The man has been changing his ways.
Autumn begins informing his song,
commencing his legacy phase.

Soon he'll turn this place over and be
accountable for what he's done.

Amy Hale Auker

He wants to leave the land bountiful,
with things growing and creeks that run.

The old cow ambles sagely and wise,
her steer trotting close by her side.
She'll bawl three days when he goes away;
in her belly, a new one rides.

A slight soft smile creases his face
as the water lot gate grows near.
That red broad with wide horns, damn she's old.
For sure he should ship her this year.

But she keeps on bringing 'em to him,
healthy calves, fat, shiny and slick.
He always finds her in those rough parts
where the best feed is strong and thick.

She leads her group in, every time,
without hint of struggle or chase.
Now at the tank, she bawls his way,
with water dripping from her face.

He closes the wire gate as he thinks;
does a quick tally in his mind.
He has shipped several old cows this fall,
and now there's room to keep her kind.

She'll show the young ones how best to move
in boulders piled high on this place,
and what to eat when it is not so good,
and where the hidden water stays.

Gentle and calm, but knows how to fight
with horns sharp and slinging snot.
The scent of coyote, lion or bear
draws memories of past battles fought.

But kind eyes rest between those wide horns,
that are wrinkled and grooved now thin.
He tosses out flakes of bright green hay,
as she brings her big steer on in.

Shaky truth he was fed in youth.
The country makes them wild, you know.
Thick brush and rocks and steep canyon walls
are not like those flats down below.

That way of thinking has now grown old.
He's had years to look at it close.
When cows run off or the creek bank's bare,
he examines his own self most.

And so he stands and watches these girls
as they chew their way through the hay.
Throws out one more fragrant bale because
he can, and it's his time of day.

SALLY BATES

Chino Valley, Arizona

Sally Bates was born in Prescott, Arizona. Her roots grew deep in Yavapai County and other parts of Arizona, on both sides of her family tree for seven generations. She started writing poetry about ranch life while still in grade school. Being homeschooled for much of her education, it was often part of her homework. At home, no electricity, no television, and rarely a transistor radio meant limited entertainment availability, so the family frequently spent time playing music and reading.

Cowgirl Karen Perkins, who nominated Sally Bates for inclusion in this book, says, "I was born and bred a ranch girl, getting my first cow horse from my great-uncle Ben when I was four. My family was made up of pioneers, driving their livestock from Fort Davis, Texas, to north-central Arizona and settling in what is now known as Perkinsville, located on the Verde River, in November 1900. This is where I, and my two kids, still live. I was very fortunate to have been born when I was, because I got to see what was left of the old West through my grandpa and the older cowboys. That was a different place and time, now long gone with the wind except in poetry, books, art, and if you are lucky, a story from someone who lived that life. As I read over some of Sally Bates's poems from her book, *Life Between Dust and Clouds*, tears fell down my face. 'The Tally Book' has to be one of my favorites. She took real excerpts from her daddy's tally book and then wrote what else happened that day that he hadn't entered."

Sally's mother and father brought her up literally singing around the "friendly campfires" of their ranch potlucks and the fireplace in their home. Her father loved Robert Service and other poets, so she frequently heard folk ballads and poetry growing up. It was that involvement and pleasure that led her to become involved with cowboy poetry gatherings around the West, and she remained a part of those events for nearly thirty years.

She has been included in five anthologies of poetry, has self-published three books of poetry, and helps other writers get their work into print. She is a songwriter, with more than one hundred songs in her portfolio and four albums of cowboy songs. Her self-published collection of ranch stories and cowboy poetry, *Life Between Dust and Clouds*, was a WILLA finalist in 2014.

She and her husband live in Chino Valley.

The Tally Book

His Levi's jumper pocket
Held a tally book inside
No matter if we went to town
Or if he had to ride
A cowboy's first day timer
I guess it could be called
'Cuz all the records he would need
Its pages would corral
He never was without it
Nor a pencil at the side
The tally book kept all his notes
On horses, rain and cowhide

Moved 47 head from Conger
Up to Seepage pasture
June the 27th
Was the date that it occurred
But what he didn't enter
On the pages of his book

Was how ten head had bolted
And his saddle horse was spooked
So he stumbled in confusion
Falling down a steep ravine
And it mashed him there
When he was caught between

Branded 60 calves today
In holding pens at Stinson
It rained about a half an inch
April 22nd
What's not here in the pages
Is that mud and cow manure
Were so thick when we were finished
We stunk like coyote lure
So when we hit headquarters
Mom was waiting at the door
Said, "Hose off out beside the shed
Don't get it on the floor."

Gave 16 shots of can milk
To 16 pink-eye cases
Stuck high horned brindle bloated up
July—screwworm cases.
What was left to memory
Was how my little mare
Got cut up on the barb-wire fence
Down thru hide and hair
We very nearly lost her
To a case of dam' screwworms
Ain't nothing stinks as bad as that!
Ain't nothin' bad as screwworms.

Found 2 heifers layin' dead
August twenty-three
Gathered 480 head
Leaves are changing early.
Tatum worked for thirty days
Got stung by a nest of bees
Charlie worked for thirty days
Ingersoll for twenty
Banker coming to appraise
Trucks the 5th of September
Mud Springs there's a Christmas tree
August 23

20 inches of new wet snow
Fell in the last seven days
23rd day of December
1978
The tally book did not record
Christmas was awesome that year
Daddy took us sledding all day
We spooked ten head of deer
And on the way home broke heavy ice
On every pond and water
I thought we'd all freeze plumb to death
Son and all four daughters.

Having chest pains thru the day
Started Charlie's roan colt
May the 2nd '78
New foal's name is Seminole
What the pages do not hold
Is that dad was not that old

Thru that week his heart was failing
We thought it was made of gold
Mom would cry—but she knew too
He had run a faithful course
'Til one day—it just exploded
Cowboy man with no remorse

He never was without one
Of these papers bound with rings
The tally book held many notes
On every little thing
And flippin' through the pages
Will quicken memories.
I wish I had those tally books
What smiles and tears they'd bring
I pray my heavenly father
Has just such a tally book
So that when we get to heaven
We can sit and take a look

Sally Bates   11

My Wild Garden

When the manzanita bells
Are ringing on the breeze
And the fragrance is heady and sweet
When the sego lily blooms
Like a treasured rare gem . . .
And the daisies are thick at my feet
When the gold of the greasewood
Blows off with the wind
As the rain fills the air with a chill
When the soft purple haze
Of the ironwood calls
And the primrose repose on the hill.
When the wild cliff roses
Are thick on the hills
And you barely can breathe it all in
When the cactus in bloom
Proves that life will resume
Even in granite and buckthorn
When the pink eye weeds
And the goldenrod
And the lupine are scattered abroad
And evening primrose
All open and close
While the sunflowers dangle and nod.
When Saguaro stand tall
With their white blossoms all
In their bower so far up above,
And the spines on their limbs

Catch the wind in its flight
And the sound is a whispering song.
Oh how I enjoy them
These days every spring
When the wildflowers waltz to the
breeze
Did I plant them, or water?
Or tend them at all?
Or simply enjoy as I please?
Oh those sweet little bells
And the colors that splash
They come with a few drops of rain
And they smile for a while
Then they dry and comply
With the change of the season again.

She Speaks to Me

For the Quiet Ones

Lift your cup of coffee brewed ... STRONG
By the stout-hearted women who
Never rode with an all-male crew
Never did what the cowboys do
Never rode the crazy broncs
Never closed a honky-tonk
Wouldn't gouge an old pink eye
Never popped mesquite brush high
Didn't want to castrate bulls
Stick a bloated cow or push
The prolapsed cow up in the chute.

Lift your cup of coffee brewed ... STRONG
And toast the quiet cowboy's wife
Mother to a motley crew
Doing what there is to do
Cooking, cleaning, making new
Packing lunch and driving to
The hold up place to feed the crew
Rising early, working late
Killing local rattlesnakes
Treating someone's pains and aches
While she thinks her back will break.

Lift your cup of coffee brewed ... STRONG
Toast the gal who's riding drag
Seeing little ones don't lag
Caring not if she's outdone
By a bull who's on the run
Happy to ride in hand-me-down

Sally Bates   13

Saddles, Stetsons and chaps all worn.
Horses she knows won't bed her down
Waiting a month to go to town
Planting her garden with prairie rose
Breaking ice on a trough that froze.

Lift your cup of coffee brewed . . . STRONG
And hold it high for the lady who
Nurtures flowers in malapa*
Builds a bang-up apple pie
Gave up on ways to beautify
Watches her wrinkles petrify
Barber, nurse and carpenter
Teacher, pastor, philosopher
Never one who rode the bronc
'Til he shivered, quit and sighed
Never in search of a glory ride.

Lift your cup of coffee brewed . . . STRONG
And hold it high for the lady who
Never had poems written for her
Never owned her own pair of spurs
Raised her kids on cockleburs
Found herself a horse chauffeur
Didn't braid a fancy coiffeur
Rarely spoke a strong cussword
Leaves no written legacy
Just makes a great cup of strong coffee
Simply rides behind the herd.

---

* Malapa are the rocks we climb through in this part of the country. Some of them get huge; some are just a pain in the hoof.
—Sally Bates

VIRGINIA BENNETT

Goldendale, Washington

Today, poet Virginia Bennett deeply misses the ranch life she once knew so intimately. Her thirty-five years on Western ranches, working alongside her husband, Pete (cowboy and ranch manager), was a time filled with hard work, often performed under extreme physical conditions. But Virginia loved every minute of it. Willing to fill in on a ranch in any way needed, she was a "range rider" on USDA Forest Service grazing allotments; broke countless young horses to ride; helped Pete pack supplies up and repair hard-to-reach fence lines; drove draft teams and took her turn checking calvy cows at midnight.

This typical ranch wife played surrogate mother to "dogie (orphan) calves"; pulled porcupine quills from dogs' muzzles; carried water from a spring to the family cabin on the Continental Divide in New Mexico; tacked on thrown horseshoes; performed life-giving CPR on a dead newborn calf; pushed stubborn cows down a narrow alleyway to the squeeze chute; and homeschooled son, Jesse, through his high school graduation, all the while keeping supper on the family table more often than not.

All of these things and more inspired her pen in the form of poetry, taking her around the country as she recited her poems and spun Western humor, until injuries from a severe "horse-wreck" ended her cowgirl career in 2004. The Academy of Western Artists honored Virginia's work and contribution to the genre of cowboy poetry with its 2014 Cowgirl Poet of the Year award. These days, Virginia and Pete care for their two dogs and two-and-a-half acres in Goldendale, Washington, and head out with their camp trailer to explore ghost towns throughout the West.

For Joelle Smith

A coyote trots with a backward glance
Along a dry ridge on a dull-gray morning.
For a moment, an eagle has flightless wings
Grounded by grief in the dreary dawning.

Miles away, a gentle, bay ranch horse,
Slowed by arthritis, too feeble to ride,
Attacks his pasture-mate, teeth bared and yellow,
Savagely dining on blood and hide.

Up north, a stock-dog crawls under the porch,
In the shadows, she cringes with wary eyes.
The lonely wind rushes in wild and scary,
Then dies down to a doldrum so the heat can rise.

In the barn, the tack-room door which never
Before jammed or stuck in any season . . .
Refuses to open, just for a moment
Like things that go awry without any reason.

For one second only, the spring turned sour,
The flowers wilted, the cabin's curtains were drawn.
The earth does mourn in sackcloth and ashes
For now we know another good cowgirl's gone.

On the Brink of Forever

I cannot explain the why of it
I barely know the how
And were it not for God's goodspeed,
I'd not be telling you now . . .

Of a hair-raising ride down Little Andrews Crik,
When the wind raised a witch's wail
As my horse stumbled over washed-out roots
and his hooves rolled rocks from the trail.

For you know, past the edge, it's damn steep,
(tho' it's so dark, your eyes ache from peerin')
when the rocks rolled off never hit bottom,
least not while you're within hearin'.

It's no time to be out in the mountains.
It's no time to be leavin' camp.
When the air is crystalled with flecks of ice,
only fool leaves fire and lamp.

But, I'd stayed out later than I thought,
Lookin' for that one, last, crazy steer.
Stubborn-pride driven, I'd searched and searched
for that brand and double-notched ear.

For the Forest Service ranger said he had spotted
a yellow steer up on a Cal Peak ledge.
For three days, I'd ridden and finally gave up
when I saw winter comin' fast over Coleman Ridge.

Virginia Bennett

Tho' I hated to do it, I knew what must be done,
to get down off that mountain, neat and quick.
For the Pasayten's unforgivin' when winter's comin' on.
So I hurried toward that trail down Little Andrews Crik.

At first, she weren't bad, as Pasayten roadways go.
She wound down just like a timber rattlesnake.
And I was mounted good, on a leggy, line-back dun.
Whatever that ol' hill'd dish out, I figgered he could take.

But the wind began to bluster and I could hear it risin' up,
Trees snappin' in the gale, and when it hit us, Dunnie staggered.
Clouds blotted out what little moonlight that we had,
And, in Nature-forced humility, I cursed myself the braggart.

I dismounted, and with bridle reins in hand,
I felt our path by inches—it was the better way.
For I knew up ahead lay the Devil's Hairpin Turn
One step straight or right, and we'd have no time to pray.

Then I stopped, in complete confusion, didn't know which way to go.
Was it my gnawin' hunger, or a tired mind unclear?
My eyes refused to focus as I tried to see the trail,
when up ahead, I thought I saw the yellow, yearling steer!

Standing on the brink of forever, he gazed off to the right.
For a long time, I figgered that was just the way to turn.
But, then he doubled left and disappeared into the snow.
If he was an apparition or not, was none of my concern.

I cast my fate onto his trail, gambling all my chips.
I was willing to trust in the route that he was picking.
We inched our way around the Devil's Hairpin Turn,
and I strained my ears far up ahead to hear his ankles clicking.

One time, I thought I'd lost him. I could see him hide nor hair.
And in the dark and the deepening snow, I could sense no track.
So, I struggled on without him, with Dunnie close behind,
his muzzle pressed up tight against my shivering back.

Then, again on a wicked corner, stood the yellow steer,
as if waiting to be sure I'd make it 'round.
As soon as I caught up to him, he continued on ahead
and I took the right just like he did and made it safe and sound.

For hours, we traveled, in this macabre dance
He'd lead and I would follow in this waltz for life and death.
And when I tripped over the rail into the Andrew's Crik corral,
I just laid there, exhausted, and finally took a ragged breath.

I spent the night in the cab of a local outfitter's truck
and Dunnie feasted on some poor hunter's hay.
In the mornin', tho' I searched, I found no further sign
of the yellow yearlin' steer who had guided out our way.

Thirty miles and three weeks later, while workin' thru the herd,
I couldn't believe my eyes when I saw a steer.
We had finished shippin' all the yearlin's, and yet I'm very sure,
He was distinctly yellow . . . and he had that familiar double-notched ear!

Songs on the Night Wind

Pennies saved on a rough-cut shelf,
safely hidden in a Log Cabin tin,
behind a Clabber Girl can, it seemed a sweet place
to be banking daydreams in.

She was the bride of a prairie pioneer,
building her home from a shanty of sod.
And each day, she labored till she was all used up,
and only inwardly questioned her God.

Each day, seeing no one but her husband,
no solace could her wounded heart find.
Grubbing out sagebrush, she even led a blind mule,
while her man, bless his heart, trudged behind.

Harder than the mule did the homesteader work.
He chased daylight from dawn till dark.
Nighttime would find him exhausted and spent,
with no strength for laughter or lark.

"You work, you survive. You don't, you die,"
was the homesteader's philosophy of life.
Too busy surviving, he couldn't perceive
the tender yearnings of his prairie wife.

So, she pored over the ragged, worn pages
of a Sears Roebuck Consumers Guide.

Yet, only one item enticed her spirit
and caused her to light up inside.

It was a canary she dreamed of
in a dandy, brass-wired cage.
A canary who'd sing softly, yet listen
to all her pent-up longings and rage.

So, she squirreled away her savings
from the sale of her Barred Rock hens' eggs,
and she sneaked in her secret Sears order
right after liniment for her husband's sore legs.

On the day the mysterious order arrived,
her husband's wrath openly vented.
For he hated (or feared) her defiant act,
and the freedom the bird represented.

But the bird, blessed with ignorance,
sang and trilled, bringing the sod shack back to life.
And each evening, in rosy glow of kerosene lamp,
a smile graced the face of the wife.

'Til the day that she ran to the cabin,
astonished at there what she'd find.
The door stood ajar, the cage door, as well.
Done either by accident or design.

Days later, she found her canary.
He lay under a tree, stone dead.
And she cried no tears as she carried him home,
for they would have been bitter tears shed.

She wrapped him a white linen hanky,
embroidered, the way wives sometimes do.
And she kept him to remember that sad day,
when out the door, her heart's melody flew.

NIKI BERG

Atlanta, Georgia

Starting out—taking the first step—can be a frightening endeavor. But not for those who feel the calling like Nicole "Niki" Berg. She packed her bags and moved from eastern Washington to Georgia to become a singer of songs that she had composed. I found her lyrics to be true and beautiful, and she has a deep, rich voice that agrees with the lyrics.

Niki was born in 1979. Some of her fondest memories growing up were of spending time with her grandparents on a ranch in eastern Washington. "I got to help my Grandpa feed the cows their early morning silage, then we'd go back to the house to get our own breakfast and coffee that Grandma flawlessly prepared." Cows, a good horse or two, and a good dog seemed to be all that was needed to define the ideal lifestyle for Niki. "I loved that place and dreaded a long week until the next weekend when I could go back and be a cowgirl again."

It's easy to see where the song "Grandpa's Old Hat" was born. Niki bounced around for awhile, but eventually settled on music, writing lyrics, and performing with her band, Rough Stock. "'Grandpa's Old Hat' is the one song that most people would say was their favorite," Niki says. "It seems a lot more people than I ever thought would find that song so relatable, and I've heard so many touching stories of an old hat or family heirloom that was passed down to them as a child by a grandfather, uncle, or father. It is a true story, it is my story.

"I really do start songs like a poem, then I play around with a melody about halfway through or so. After that I can usually feel what direction the song is going, then finish. I hope this all makes sense?"

Reading her poetic lyric, yes, it does, Niki.

Grandpa's Old Hat

Dust on the brim, sweat stain on the band
I'd put that old hat on and be the shadow at his right hand
Grandma said, "Put a finger in his belt loop so your little legs keep up"
All three feet of me was walking tall and proud as I ran and jumped in his truck

Chorus:
'Cause Grandpa gave me his old hat
and nothing in the world at the time was more special than that
He didn't show off, he didn't pretend
He was teacher and protector, the strongest of men
And I thank God for that
And the memories in Grandpa's old hat

Mama said, "Throw that old thing away, stop covering your pretty curls"
But my hero, he gave it to me, it was my favorite treasure in the world
It was way too big and the grown-ups they made fun of me
But under that old hat I was exactly who I wanted to be

Chorus

No Matter Where You Go

No matter where you go, there you are
You can try to outrun yourself, but you won't get very far
Sometimes it feels like I can't get out of my own way
I'll stop tripping over my own feet someday

I've gotta break myself out of this box
Because the payoff isn't nearly worth the cost
I look in the mirror and don't believe what I see
There's nothing left but a shadow of me

Well, I can hop on a westbound plane
Find a taxicab or a train
But the destination always seems the same

Better days have got to be in store for me
I just gotta figure out exactly what I need
It's time I started taking my own advice
And create, believe, receive instead of rolling these evil dice

'Cause I can hop on a westbound plane
Find a taxicab or a train
But the destination always seems the same

'Cause no matter where you go, there you are
You can try to outrun yourself, but you won't get very damn far
Sometimes it feels like I can't get out of my own way
I'll stop tripping over my own feet someday
I'll stop tripping over my own feet someday . . .

TERESA BURLESON

Weatherford, Texas

Teresa Burleson is an award-winning cowgirl poet whose poems are inspired by her personal experiences, her heritage, and the Western way of life. That she has an appreciation for the agricultural industry and the people who make their lives in it is clear in her poetry, as well as in her zest for life and in her ability to make people laugh and to touch their lives.

With a clear, soft Texas drawl and a voice that cowboy poet Waddie Mitchell once declared was "like silk," her poetry is beautiful, soulful, and aimed straight for the Western heart (or the funny bone) as she tells of drought, rain, loss, faith, pride, legacy, nature, horses, calving, and all the joys and hazards in life.

Tammy Goldammer, a rancher and blogger in Missouri, chose Teresa Burleson's "Rhythms" as her favorite because every line "specifically relates to my entire life growing up as a rancher's daughter in the Sandhills of Nebraska in the 1960s. Every single line, every single word of the poem 'Rhythms' touches every fiber of my being. It is like 'Rhythms' is written for me, about me."

Teresa was one of 2014's top five nominees for Female Poet of the Year with the Western Music Association (WMA). In 2013, she was also among the top five nominees for Female Poet of the Year with the WMA. In 2010, she was awarded the Cowgirl Poet of the Year by the Academy of Western Artists. Her first CD, *The Cowgirl Way*, was released in 2009. Her second CD, *The Legend Remains*, was released in August 2013.

> Ride tall in the saddle and pull yer hat low,
> Let the Lord ride with you where'er you may go!
>
> —Teresa Burleson

Rhythms

God gave us each a tempo that's keeping time with His spirit.
So we can sing along with Him and let the rest of the world hear it.

My life is made up of rhythms that began with the beat of a heart.
The spirit of man and the elements of land each play an equal part.

Listen close and you'll hear a tune played by the cattle as they graze,
The chewing of cud and swishing of tail wile away the summer days.

I hear the creaking windmill keeping time with the song of the wind,
The wind that is blowing in the clouds that are rain's next of kin.

And the beat of those raindrops falling on the roof made of tin,
Bringing the nourishment that will make the prairie dance again.

Or the blatant contrast and the stillness of a hot August drought,
As the pulse of the heat that is bearing down and drying out.

I've danced to the cadence of a horse and the fall of its hooves,
I have sat atop the power and become one with its moves.

It's a ride that beats out a rhythm that fulfills a spiritual need,
And I know the calming measure and meter of my horse eating its feed.

I've experienced the flow of memories that rush in to flood my mind,
They transport me to another place and the lyrics of another time.

I recall the beat of the pots and pans from momma in the kitchen,
As she bustles around, peeling potatoes and frying up the chicken.

Teresa Burleson

27

And there's the rhythm and the urgency of a newborn baby's cry,
Accompanied by the soft, soothing whisper of a mother's lullaby.

Yes, life is full of rhythms, like the lilt of laughter and the flow of tears.
The song may change but the beat remains as I waltz through the years.

Each rhythm has made me who I am and brought me to this place and time.
Each beat has fulfilled a destiny that is so uniquely mine.

The love of the West and all that it holds is a symphony within my spirit.
God has put a poem in my heart and I want the rest of the world to hear it.

She Speaks to Me

The Investment

He's a rowdy six-year-old and his mama's pride and joy.
He looks like his daddy did when he was a little boy.

His hat sits low, atop his ears and the brim's a little bent.
Beneath it are brown eyes, freckled face and a nose that is skint.

His shirt is buttoned to the top like his daddy does.
There's a trophy buckle at his waist and a pair of leather gloves.

He wears hand-me-down boots with tall tops that are blue.
His jeans are tucked inside 'em like the other punchers do.

He sure looks like a cowboy and that's what he wants to be.
But there's much more to him than the clothes that you see.

He's already learning honor and treats his elders with respect.
It's a pride in what he stands for and just what mom expects.

He's not impressed by celebrities who have fortune and fame.
His daddy is his hero and he proudly shares his name.

He helps with the spring works and again at the fall gathers.
He looks forward to the fun and he's learnin' what matters.

When he's bigger he'll flank 'em and stretch 'em out when they brand.
For now, he will do what he can and he'll try to make a hand.

Teresa Burleson

Growing up a ranch kid teaches the value of work and play.
His parents watch with pride as he takes up the cowboy way.

They know you have to let 'em try and let 'em have a turn,
And if you don't take 'em with you they will never learn.

He is cherished with a gentle love that is kind and firm,
And when needed, disciplined with a hand that is stern.

This little boy is an investment in a heritage and tradition.
To teach a child the way to go is a God-given commission.

Now, he may choose a different path than the one his parents sought,
But he'll always have the ethics and the values he's been taught.

Right now, he is only six years old but one day he'll understand,
It ain't all about being a cowboy, it's about being a good man.

The Calf Book

Wash day . . . it's not my favorite thing to do but a necessary chore.
Sortin' colors from whites, dainties from jeans, making piles on the floor.

And emptying my husband's pockets 'cause there's no tellin' what they hide,
Double-check those coveralls 'cause they have secret pockets inside.

I've been known to launder money with that forgotten dollar bill.
One day I washed a palpation glove and a bovine sulphur pill.

I've washed pliers, fencing steeples, hay, and receipts for feed and lumber.
And I mistakenly thought I'd washed another woman's number.

I've laundered the errant glove, syringe, ear tag and even a blue ink pen.
But that ruined my favorite shirt and I'll never do that again.

Then one day my greatest fear came upon me, I hate to even tell!
There, in the washer, was the equivalent to the Holy Grail!

The Calf Book! I washed the precious Calf Book! You know the one I mean.
The cowman's diary of breeding, calving and everything in between.

That pocket notebook with all the facts a rancher writes about cows.
Like which number heifer was bred to which bull, on what day and how.

Teresa Burleson

Which black cow had what black calf and how to tell the difference.
Which bull's in what pasture and each one's scrotal circumference.

There it was, tattered, smeared, and the pages looked really thin.
The little that was left of it had survived the wash, rinse and spin.

My first impulse was to hide it but that would be deceiving.
I thought maybe I should run but I couldn't see me leaving.

Then I figured, "I'm not to blame! It's his pocket, it's not my fault!"
Just because I do the laundry am I guilty by default?

I gathered up the pieces and my nerve and gave him the soggy mess.
He looked at me kinda funny when he realized my stress.

He asked me why I was distraught and on the verge of tears,
"There's no need to be upset," he said, "this Calf Book is last year's!"

I couldn't believe what I was hearing and I admit I was relieved.
But I almost had a heart attack and that left me a little peeved.

Didn't he understand my panic when I thought I'd washed his book?
Couldn't he see my concern when he gave me that funny look?

Then and there we came to an agreement and he didn't even scoff.
He would check the pockets of dirty clothes before he took them off.

From now on if the things in his pocket end up in the laundry,
It will be his responsibility and won't leave me in a quandary.

She Speaks to Me

DORIS DALEY

Black Diamond, Alberta, Canada

A sense of humor always tickles me. This poet wrote, when asked, a wonderfully amusing description of herself:

"Doris Daley is a ranch-raised, grass-fed, windblown, puffed and powdered, frocked and fringed, hale and hearty, happy-trailed, spangled and wrangled road warrior, wordsmith and Western poet."

Twice voted top female cowboy poet in North America, Doris appears frequently on stages large and small, wherever friends of the West gather throughout Canada and the United States. Her poetry is a reflection of the contemporary West and stems from her roots growing up on a fifth-generation, 130-year-old ranch in Alberta's foothills.

Prepare to be tickled reading her poetry. I certainly was—especially the line, "Heck, it takes me eighteen seconds just to swing my right leg up." Talk about relating!

Average Girl

I'd boast about my calf crop but I had to sell my cows
If you saw me on a gather you'd be right to raise your brows.
I never ran the barrels even when I was a pup.
Heck, it takes me 18 seconds just to swing my right leg up.

I never won a buckle and I never roped a bear.
I can't set a decent post; I don't wear Carhartt's underwear.
My stock dog is a Labrador; my chore truck is a Rav.
Rocketbusters are a luxury I know I'll never have.

I don't own Garcia spurs; I'm Joe Average, I admit.
I can't throw the hoolihan; heck, I can barely throw a fit.
I'm not so hot reversing if a trailer's on behind.
If you pick me last for roping, I assure you I won't mind.

When they're calling for the buckaroos, I'll never make the cut
Goodness knows I'd strut my stuff but I have no stuff to strut.
I'm Average Girl! The one whose cowboy skills are pretty thin,
Still, when they're rounding up the Westerners, I hope they'll count me in.

Songs are rightly sung about the exploits of the great.
Me—I'm just thrilled to tag along, content to get the gate.
Who sings a cowboy anthem for the average Jack and Jill?
What page is spilled with ink from the cowboy poet's quill?

Here's a toast to all us plodders who will never lead the race.
We're barely worth our porridge but our heart's in the right place.
We're the first to stand and cheer when the experts do their best
We don't sparkle, flash or dazzle, we're just glad to live out West.

For each mediocre rider, for each average girl and guy
I say, Thank you God for placing us beneath a Western sky.
In my case, being average has turned out to be a perk:
I just get to wear the clothes 'cause no one wants me for my work!

A Real Partner

My name is Guy Weadick, how do you do?
A pleasure to meet you, Miss Flores LaDue!
The horses are saddled, would you care for a ride?
I'd love to step out with you by my side.
I'll tell you my dreams about a big Wild West show.
I'm throwing a big loop by the banks of the Bow.

Mr. Weadick, I'm told, you talk big and bold.
That's fine with me, 'cause ordinary leaves me cold.
I'd love to go riding, as it happens I'm free
Any horse that has hair is just dandy with me.
I've had my eye on you from the start
When you're throwing your loop, you might aim for my heart.

She had her trick rope and he had a dream,
They aimed for the stars and they pulled as a team.
With sparkle and spunk they could conquer the world.
A gamble, a promise, a plan was unfurled.
They rode side by side and they rode to succeed,
And they did it! They started the Calgary Stampede.

A daring-do husband, a plucky young wife
Hell-bent for leather, lived larger than life.
They were partners in work and partners in play
They rode by a standard that lives on today.
A heart full of Try. A world full of Yes . . .
A legacy branded the C Lazy S.

Doris Daley

1951, her last setting sun.
Her saddle is empty, her last race is run.
A cowboy heads west, a grave stands alone
Three little words are carved on a stone.
Three little words, but they stand true and tall:
A Real Partner, and that, in the West, says it all.

My Million Star Resort

Five-star accommodations, said the Duke of La-di-Da
To stay in less would simply be unthinkable, n'est-ce pas?
Valet parking, chandeliers and a million-dollar view . . .
Security must be discreet, the fixtures must be new.

Exclusive and deluxe, agreed the Nabob of Bel Air
Marble tile in the ensuite, Persian rugs upon the stair.
The sheets must be 800 count, the duchess needs her spa
And by the bed, a basket with champagne and caviah.

To each his own, I figure. Every kettle has its lid.
But a fancy five-star penthouse isn't even on my grid.
A suite at Hotel Hoity Toit just doesn't light my lamp
'Cause nothing holds a candle to a skookum mountain camp.

Where the rooms are made of canvas with a nifty zippered door.
A scattering of mud and needles decorate the floor.
The coffee is outstanding, the cuisine is simply great:
When you're hungry, beans and bacon are perfection on your plate.

Dimensions of the en suite are modest, it is true.
But when you're sitting sweetly on it, it's a billion-dollar view.
Marble is redundant at the best seat on the planet—
It's a Rocky Mountain vista that we never take for granite.

The help is sometimes snuffy, but tough as mountain goats
All it takes to keep them happy is a morning feed of oats.
Security is peerless in our little mountain den,
The dog will bark when bears come close . . . nine times out of ten.

And when the sun begins to melt behind the western rim,
A choir of coyotes sings its wild soprano hymn.
The fire crackles brightly; the stars are all at play
Our little camp lies sparkling beneath the Milky Way.

Then I think about the jet set, those dukes and bon vivants
Wrapped up in silk and satin in their measly five-star haunts.
Nine hundred and ninety-nine thousand, nine-hundred ninety-five short
To come close to what I have, here at my million star resort.

Doris Daley

JANICE GILBERTSON

King City, California

Janice Gilbertson writes within the traditional cowboy style of metered-and-rhymed verse, but her lovely poetry is filled with descriptions portraying scenes of her childhood spent on the family ranch where her father eked out a simple life, grazing his cattle nearby in the Santa Lucia Mountains—"The Lucias," west of King City, California, in an area known as part of "John Steinbeck Country." From those early days, Janice has penned many well-crafted poems and two Western novels. Janice still makes her home in the foothills of the Santa Lucia range with her husband, Ron, and can often be found riding her mustang mare along well-known trails.

Virginia Bennett, who nominated Janice, says, "The way I see it, there is no limit to what this gal can do with words in her heart and a pen in her hand."

Janice has been writing and sharing cowboy and Western poetry for more than twenty years. Her poetry book's title poem, "Sometimes, in the Lucias" (included here), was named a Western Writers of America Spur Finalist in 2009. Her debut novel, *Summer of '58*, was recently published by Pen-L Publishing.

Nighttime's Promise

Let's ride at night through a blue shadowed canyon under a night-light sky
Let's choose a trail that is North Star-bound under a high moon's watchful eye

Ride your best horse and I'll ride mine too, and we'll trust them to travel a surefooted trail
Let's use fancy spurs we've been saving for someday and silver bridles that hang from a nail

Let's laugh at old stories, sing old cowboy songs and share hopes for time still ahead
We'll shed daylight worries, sad thoughts and bad thoughts and wrong things that somebody said

Let's take this ride together, giddy on fancy and freedom and dreams
Let's shoot for the stars up that silver-lit trail, track promise by the light of moonbeams

We'll ride a good ride through the nighttime air t'ward the renewing dawn
With rein chains swingin' and spur rowels a jinglin', let's meet the new day head-on

Janice Gilbertson

Sometimes, in the Lucias

Sometimes—on a ridge in the hard, hot air where deer hooves clatter on chalk
Horned toads hide in plain view and jackrabbit trembles in shadow of hawk

Sometimes—I hear sounds, bees on the sage the ever-singing gnat at my ear
The music of shifting, falling shale 'neath the pads of something wild come near

From the time I was just a small child I rode long days out on my own
I wonder, now, at my soulful comfort perhaps I never was really alone

Sometimes—it is voices I hear not words, but the sounds of words
That rise from canyon shadow or fly through the air with swifting birds

I can hear the thrum of man-talk and the melody of women's voices high
Children's giggles with the singing gnat infants fuss in spotted fawn's cry

If I leave the ridge to ride the trail to where a spring flows sweet and free
Sometimes—when my lips touch the pool, the reflection there is not of me

The mountains of Lucia harbor spirits of those who came here long before
And sometimes, now, I follow the trails of Padres, Salinans and Conquistadors

How I long to sit with them beside a shady, singing willow creek
Or ride beside a spirit horse up-trail to a glorious coastal peak

They beckon me to painted caves. they welcome me to adobe walls
And though we share no common blood there is a sort of kin who calls . . .

Sometimes—I lay in silent dark and ask, should I ever ride away
Though I may go with heart and soul will my spirit choose to stay?

Giving In to Lonesome

Her long legs, bony knees poking
At pant legs, sun-bleached and threadbare
Disappear into his knee-high boots with
Burlap-stuffed toes, and worn beyond repair

Her bare hands no longer noticing the cold
Are bent and fused until they feel no pain
The right rested in its place on her thigh
The left hand's crooked fingers weave the rein

It is his tattered sheepskin coat she wears
Unbuttoned to the cold, early morning air
And it is his ole blue scarf 'round her throat
Shaped by his sweat and the knot he'd tied there

She quietly sits her beloved bay gelding
Narrow-chested and slightly splayed
He is stoved and gaunt with age
Hipbones wide and back some swayed

They stand for a moment just inside the gate
Both shifting old bodies for comfort's sake
She legs his ribby side gently and turns
To ride the ancient fence north to the break

'Neath a cast-iron sky without a glint of star
She rides through the dark before dawn
By the instincts of a thousand rides
They travel by memory of days bygone

Janice Gilbertson

There was a time she rode here on snorty colts
Their morning-fresh stride dancing her along
What a grand time she would have then,
Looking for that stray where it didn't belong

There are no cattle now, not for a decade
But old habits hang on like old barbed wire
His fence pliers still hang in their scabbard
To twist a wire, tap a staple, should she desire

Ghost calves bawl for want of their mamas
Bulls bellow for long-gone cows on the lowland
She sees him on his black on the zigzag trail
Where he is sitting his saddle just grand!

Time's trickery confuses her and she curses
At her old mind where his image lingers
Ghostly fog knuckles over the ridge
Crawls the canyons in cold, grey fingers

A harsh chill shudders her thin body
And sends gooseflesh down her spine
The familiar sounds and images
So cruelly tease her lonesome mind

For the first time she turns back on her trail
Finally . . . leaving her life as it were
For the very first time in fifty years
She leaves the gate stand open behind her

AUDREY HANKINS

Skull Valley, Arizona

Audrey Hankins is an Arizona ranch wife who, like some horses and dogs, was born with "cow" in her heart. In her words: "I've been blessed to spend most of my life connected to the land, the livestock and people who live on it.

"I love poetry, the way words ring off each other and take on power in certain combinations, so it's natural to combine my loves by writing. Many of my poems are memorials to specific horses, dogs, cattle, places, and people that have enriched my life.

"Through the years, cowboy poetry and music have drawn together those of us whose hearts beat strong for this way of life. Geographically, we're a far-flung group; but emotionally we are kindred souls."

What a lovely thought that is—kindred souls.

Some Things Never Change

Some things never change
And I like it that way.
Things I can depend on—
Like night follows day.

Seedtime and harvest, cold and heat,
Summer and winter, Nature's ways,
Ever new, yet always the same
Cycles of life that order my days.

Spring coming every year,
With baby calves and brand new hope.
The all-day strength of an honest horse,
The usefulness of nylon rope.

The independent spirit
Of folks who love the land.
A quiet pride in self-reliance,
Ridin' for the brand.

Heat and dust and burning hair,
They're all part of a whole.
The never-changing elements
Of a life that is part of my soul.

I love some things that never change—
Birds twittering at first light.
Cottonwood leaves rustling in a breeze,
A familiar trail on a moonlit night.

The scent of greasewood after rain,
A fresh clean wind across the range.
The kingdom, the power, the glory—
Thank God for things that never change.

Cattle and Horses

Cattle and horses, cattle and horses,
The musical sound of the phrase—
Conjures up colorful images
Of brindles and gleaming bays.

Babysitter mama cows, shiny red calves,
Trotty old drys, a belligerent bull,
Solid ranch horses, curious colts,
Mother mares, their manes blowing full.

Cattle and horses, cattle and horses,
Constant through all my days.
The source of wrecks and broken bones,
As I strive to learn their ways.

Cattle, the reason for my favorite work,
Horses, the way to get it done,
Cornerstones under a way of life
That's a tough but satisfying one.

Cattle and horses trotted and loped
Through all my little-girl dreams.
Someday they'll thread a meandering trail
Through an old woman's memories.

Audrey Hankins

In Our Blood

Why love our desert ranches,
Rundown, remote, and dry?
Ask any of us that question,
It's hard to answer why.

It's not just cattle and horses,
The land is in our blood.
Our pores are choked with alkali
Our veins bleed 'dobe mud.

Our skin is leather from furnace winds
Sweeping out of white-hot sky.
Our hair is hoary with dust
When whirlwinds come tearing by.

But our eyes see shimmering images,
Dancing to faraway butte.
Our ears are tuned to ring of spur—
Music from high-heeled boot.

Our souls are soothed by winter rain,
Water running everywhere.
Full tanks, "filaree," Indian wheat,
Baby calves replace despair.

This land both grips and repels us.
It's home of the buzzard and dove.
When we leave, something compels us
To return. It's the land that we love.

She Speaks to Me

JONI HARMS

Canby, Oregon

Singer/songwriter Joni Harms says this about herself, "I personally can't live without Western music. I like a lot of today's country music, but the truth of the matter is that I'm very serious about keeping the Western side of country music alive." The sincerity in her voice is clear.

"The majority of my songs include lyrics of the West, because I love to write about things I've experienced," she says. "Rodeo, cowboys, and the ranch way of living shows through a lot in my music."

Joni Harms is no stranger to success. She has been a winner of multiple Academy of Western Artists Awards, including top honor for Entertainer of the Year in 2002. In 2003, Harms was named Female Vocalist of the Year, and accepted the award for Song of the Year from the Western Music Association. She continues building audiences through appearances at the famed Grand Ole Opry, and even an appearance at New York City's Carnegie Hall.

Joni lives with her family on a ranch in Oregon that was homesteaded by her great-great-grandfather in 1872, and this has been an inspiration for many of her songs. Joni says, "I always want the songs I sing to be a good representation of who I am."

Long Hard Ride

Taking care of the cattle
With frost on my saddle
They're watered and well fed tonight
There's a new calf a'bawlin'
A light snow's a'fallin'
And it's been a long hard ride

Now I'm headin' for home
Where I know it's safe and warm
Chores over and I'm satisfied
Sit back, drop the reins
My horse knows the way
After a long hard ride

Way out here tonight
The stars shine so bright
Lord, what a beautiful land
It's no mystery
It's easy to see
This was painted by the master's hand

And when he calls me home
I'll be safe and warm
Chores over and I'm satisfied
Sit back, drop the reins
The Lord knows the way
After a long hard ride

Lord, it's been a long hard ride.

She Speaks to Me

LINDA HASSELSTROM

Hermosa, South Dakota

When a well-known poet speaks of another poet's work as "breathtaking," I know it must be very good. When you read the poems of Linda Hasselstrom, I know you will agree. (Here is a little hint: Read the last one aloud.)

Linda Hasselstrom is a South Dakota rancher who has roamed across miles of grassland with no company but her horse. She is the full-time resident writer at Windbreak House Retreats, established in 1996. Her writing has appeared in dozens of anthologies and magazines. *Dirt Songs: A Plains Duet*, with Twyla M. Hansen, won the Nebraska Book Award for Poetry in 2012, and was a finalist for both a High Plains Book Awards and Women Writing the West's WILLA award. *Bitter Creek Junction* won the Wrangler for Best Poetry from the National Cowboy & Western Heritage Museum in Oklahoma City, Oklahoma. *No Place Like Home: Notes from a Western Life* won the 2010 WILLA in creative nonfiction.

Formerly visiting faculty for Iowa State University in Ames, Iowa, and online mentor for the University of Minnesota's Split Rock writing program, Linda is an advisor to Texas Tech University Press.

Learning About Gates

Always shut the gate behind you,
he taught me first when I was ten.
He showed me how to squeeze hard
and yank the wire loop up. Before
my muscles grew, he let me use
the wire stretcher on the tight ones.
When we moved cows to summer pasture,
he'd drive the pickup ahead, open each gate,

count the cattle through while I followed
on my horse. He'd shut that gate, idle
the truck past, being sure each cow's calf
was next to her; open the next gate.

    He didn't go to church.
He put his faith in keeping fences tight
and four wires high; in shutting gates
and paying bills. He believed in buffalo grass
and rain in June. He didn't trust anyone
who couldn't look him in the eye or shake
his hand. He said, "My shadow on this place
is worth forty dollars a day."

    At his funeral, the minister said
God planted a garden over east in Eden,
and created ranching when He made a woman.
My neighbor Margaret told me,
"He's gone ahead to open the gates."

Gate Keeper, whether your gate's gold
or barbed wire, you can trust my dad
to count them through.

Where I'm From

I.

I come from
black widow spiders under the porch,
and strawberries dipped in sugar.
I come from
gold-lit windows in the long train at night,
and buffalo grass on graves.

I come from
graveled trails to the ranch in the canyon
where I polished kerosene lamps.
I come from
chicken fried on a wood-fired stove,
and a trail to the outhouse behind.

I come from
skinned knees, and grandma crocheting
after we lit the lamps.
I come from
western boots and country school,
and neighbors dropping by.

I come from
Cora and Harry, from Millie and John,
tomatoes and corn in the garden.
I come from
home-canned beef and chicken soup,
from Sunday church with Mother while Father
mowed and raked and stacked his prayers.

II.

I'm headed home
to grassfed beef and chicken soup,
to dandy ice cream and devil's food cake.
I'm headed home
to coyote howls and red-tailed hawks
perched on cedar posts.

I'm headed home
to gravel roads, and mail stuffed
into a highway box;
I'm headed home
to cattle trotting down the ridge,
to jingling spurs, whirling ropes and branding fires.

I'm headed home
to folks who knew my father's dad,
whose grandmothers knew mine,
and to the cemetery where they wait,
in graves that grow buffalo grass.

Linda Hasselstrom

A Venue of Vultures

Seventeen vultures perched all night
in the dead tree beside the gas station.
This morning I see them circling,
circling over the city, a kettle
on the boil.

     Shivering
in September's sunrise, I pick
orange tomatoes beaded with moisture
—not quite frost, but close.
Fingers tingling, I align them
on the shelf under the kitchen window.
The clock says it's time to go.

In a car the color of fog I head north,
breathing deep, remembering the fall day
my husband and I saw twenty-three vultures
settle in the cottonwood beside my parents' house.
We all joked about the omens. Now
he's buried near my folks, closer
on cemetery hill than they were in life.

Still alive myself, I snap
Patsy Cline into the tape deck, hum
with Emmylou and Nanci Griffith,
hammer on the steering wheel,
bruising my hands to feel the bass.
Those women sing me through

this autumn sunlight, spin me toward
the rolling winter clouds.
We sing because we can.
We sing because we live.

Near the ranch, another sagging roof
has fallen in; another subdivision's
windows and garages gape above
the buffalo grass they will displace.
Blackbirds slide between the clouds,
wings so close they seem to brush my hair.
The grass glints yellow, green, brown,
green, red, green, brown, gone.

Autumn does this to me every time.
So many of the ones I've loved have died
as summer faded: grandmother, mother
father, best friend, husband. Sometimes
I dream of children.
There a pronghorn buck runs younger males
away from his band of does.
Yesterday I savored the last
tart rose hip on the bush. And there—
I count fast: twenty-four buzzards
jostle on that roadkill deer.

Here comes another fall
when I'm not settled where I want to die,
where I will watch leaves drop, snow sift down,

rain and sunlight come
again and again and again,
until I know in every bone the day
the swallows will come back.
I want to tuck myself into that hillside
where I've loved and lost
and loved some more,
and keep right on living. Make
the buzzards wait.

Linda Hasselstrom

JESSICA HEDGES

Lovelock, Nevada

Jennifer Dennison, senior editor of *Western Horseman* magazine, first met this poet at the ranch Jessica and her husband, Sam, were running in Oregon in 2011 for an article that appeared in *Western Horseman* and then again at the National Cowboy Poetry Gathering in Elko, Nevada, in January 2013. She has this to say about Jessica Hedges's poetry:

"Some poets write and recite classic poems about the past, and some spin satirical stories into humorous rhymes. Jessica Hedges writes about real-life situations she experiences as a ranch hand's wife and a mother of two young sons living on outfits in the Great Basin. She sees the humor and hardships associated with ranch life and writes with a sincere sensitivity for the land, livestock, and rural traditions. An ambassador for the rancher, Jessica strives to take her and her husband's everyday activities, whether somber or comical, and convey them in a way in which her audience can relate and see that the West is still alive, just not where everyone can witness it."

I will only add that Jennifer Hedges was the first "cowgirl" poet I ever heard, and she got me started on this project.

Listening for His Cinch Bell
Dear Lord, I know I don't talk with you enough
Here anymore, it's just because he is late
I always knew his days would be long and tough
But I didn't know how hard it'd be to wait

It's two hours past dark, four past quitting time
He should have been home by now, where's he at?
A storm's coming on; I can hear my wind chimes
About then, the first raindrop falls with a splat

He mentioned he was checking heifers today
Up in the high pasture, the one past the creek
He was going to trot out, thought he'd take the grey
That raunchy one, you know, that has the mean streak

I know I shouldn't worry, but yet I do
He's a big boy, he can take care of himself
His absence continues to make my mind stew
Could he be hiding beneath the rocky shelf?

Maybe that no good colt tipped over on him?
Maybe those heifers are scattered all around
From heck to breakfast out on that shell rock rim?
And maybe, he's lying wounded on the ground?

At the door, I strain to hear his jingle bobs
Regardless of the brewing storm just outside
This is the downfall of these cowboying jobs
Peering into the dark, looking for his stride

Lord, please quiet my mind and ease this girl's heart
For the sake of my sanity, send him home
As his wife, I've always tried to do my part
I promised from his side I would not roam

The dog perks his ears and heads toward the front door
I can hear it too; his cinch bell ringing
And comes the end of my internal war
This time, but the battle wounds are still stinging.

Jessica Hedges

Riding Tall

There was a time I'd say try me
Never afraid of being bucked down
Long trotting horses could set me free
Regardless of my husband's frown

But time went on and the babies came
Promising I wouldn't safety up
And although I refused to be tame
I'd lost that adventure of a pup

One compromise and then another
A branding season without a hope
My first job was being a mother
Obligations came before my rope

My former glory all but forgot
When I rode big horses and nice spades
Pride in things that could never be bought
Where love and time were supporting aids

Now I yearn for my sons to know
The title mom isn't my bio
How deep and wild my passion flows
How trotting out makes my heart glow

Will they see the sacrifice I made
Or just a desperate clinging attempt
To hang onto the life I portrayed
Or worse, think that they are my contempt

I'd trade every day a horseback
I've ever had to do this again
Sell every bit of silver and tack
For a chance that they'd become great men

Nah, I guess I haven't lost my nerve
Just reprioritized things is all
For it's a privilege to get to serve
As mother when I see my boys riding tall

Making Cattle Grow

One staple on every ranch is a freezer full of beef
And honestly that assurance is quite a relief

But because it is your protein source each and every day
You may need a break. All things in moderation they say

Due to this, on the rare occasion I can eat in town
It will be chicken, seafood or pork on my plate, hands down

Now I've had more than one critic ask me my reason why
I don't support the product that's my fiscal supply

I always have to laugh at this, they really just don't know
The blood, sweat, and tears I've put into making cattle grow

Like breaking ice with the chisel end of a tamping bar
By sane folks' standards don't make you a superstar

Shivering in pajamas at two a.m. in the barn
Pulling a calf and saying a lot worse than "oh gosh darn"

They've never choked on bug dust while out riding the drag
Being out all night on fire watch isn't much to brag

I'm sure they have the image of Roy Rogers and Trigger
But the jug-headed string horse I'm riding takes more rigor

Excuse me if I don't put my money where my mouth is
Because your actions speak louder than green stuff in this biz

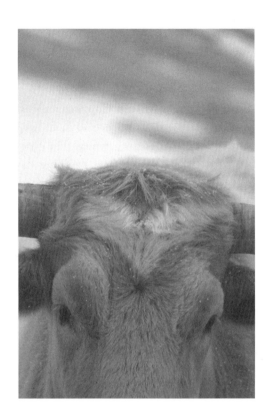

DEBRA COPPINGER HILL

Chelsea, Oklahoma

Debra Coppinger Hill lives in rural Rogers County, Oklahoma, just north of Chelsea on the border of Catale. She is the ranch manager for the family operation, the 4DH Ranch, where they raise cutting and ranch-bred horses, hay, and Brahma-cross cattle. She draws from her daily experiences, giving her writing a "been there, done that" quality to which her readers can relate. In 2002 the Academy of Western Artists named Debra the Best Female Poet of the Year. Her column, "Ridin' Drag," featured stories about her life on the ranch, as well as stories about Western history.

Her love of Western literature and writing was fostered by her grandfathers and great-grandfathers. From them, she heard tales of Texas and of being a cowboy, as well as the stories of the Cherokees.

Debra also attributes her love of stories of the past to the rest of her family, who all love to tell and retell family and Indian lore. She says, "Having lived in various parts of the country before returning to Oklahoma, I have found that most people will respond to a piece of writing if it reminds them of home or family." She believes all families should share their histories because, "in looking back, we can see more clearly where to go. A common history is what defines family and country. After all, we make the world we live in. For good things to survive, we have to take on the responsibility of promoting their positive aspects. It is our duty and our sacred trust."

Swapping Spirits

She said, "I can't explain it,
there are no words, of course,
for that moment when you're training,
when you truly connect with the horse.

Everything comes together,
it sets your soul to reeling,
you either 'get it' or you don't,
it's an indescribable feeling.

So, call it Swapping Spirits,
because nothing can compare,
to when you are the horse and the horse is you,
and you're breathing the same air."

Debra Coppinger Hill

Common Sense, Men and Horses

We perched atop the corral,
 as he read the men and horses,
And he told me about common sense
 and it's amazing, magical forces.

We watched the men choose their mounts,
 some were firm, but kind,
While others used plain brute force,
 to make their horses mind.

He said, "Dealing with horses and people
 is a special kind of art.
If you watch 'em work, you'll learn
 what is truly in a man's heart.

For though it once was common place,
 common sense ain't common any more
And many of the basic rules of life,
 some folks will choose to ignore.

The truth is just as obvious
 as these fellows working the pens.
There will always be Cowboys
 as long as there are horses and men.

And just as it takes all kinds of horses,
 from renegades to leaders to make a herd,
There will also always be outlaws
 as well as men true to their word.

You see, a man who can't,
    will often bully his way through,
And how a man treats his horse
    is how he'll end up treating you.

The decisions that we make
    should be rooted in our common sense.
Like horses, we should use our instincts,
    or be prepared to accept the consequence."

We watched 'em work for hours,
    as I hung on every word he had to say;
About life, love and horses;
    how God hears us when we pray.

I simply took it for granted
    that he would always be,
Sitting on that fence rail,
    talking and laughing with me.

Debra Coppinger Hill

Time makes changes as it passes by,
 I grew up and followed my star;
But in times of trouble I'd hear his voice,
 saying "Remember who's child you are."

He taught me to read the world
 though I didn't know it at the time.
I learned about strength and self-respect,
 how to recognize the best in mankind.

Oh, I made mistakes, but have no regrets,
 for each is valuable in its own way,
Combined with his words and an education,
 they are a part of who I am today.

So I honor this Cowboy philosopher,
 who taught me to follow my heart's voice;
To see things exactly for what they are
 and that happiness is a choice.

And nothing ever really gets me down,
 because of these things I can be sure;
That home is where the heart is,
 and that love will forever endure.

I realize all those things I learned,
 from books and college courses,
Will never hold a candle to his lesson,
 On common sense and men and horses.

The Edge

"It will be a Long-day,"
you would say, as you checked the cinch,
and with that I would know
not to expect you,
until darkness had begun.

Into the tall grass
you would ride.
And I, left here,
set the cabin straight,
and fed and watered and gathered eggs.

On the Long-days,
we lived in two worlds.
Yours, an open prairie covered in cattle.
Mine, a homestead covered in dust.

I often wondered
if the wind that so tormented me,
was the same wind
that you spoke of as magical.

I did not love this world then.
I loved only you.
And it was you,
and you alone,
who made it bearable.

On the Long-days,
knowing you would come back
tired, yet satisfied and pleased,
I wrote the letters to the family,
and lied about the love
I had for this place.

Then, you did not ride in.
They found the broken shell of you,
the horse dead too,
where you shot it to save its suffering.
Never mind, that you suffered also.

Family and friends tell me
that this place is too much for me alone.
But I cannot . . . and will not, leave.

This place owes me your spirit.
And I will wait here,
until it comes in the wind
and pushes the dust away.

Until it picks me up,
and dances me across the prairie,
and into your arms;

At the edge of the darkness
where you ride,
at the end
of a Long-day.

YVONNE HOLLENBECK

Clearfield, South Dakota

Getting to know Yvonne Hollenbeck was easy. We fell right into a long, easy conversation, and I felt like I had known her for years.

Yvonne Hollenbeck was born and raised in the Nebraska Panhandle. "All of my relatives and ancestors have either been farmers or ranchers on the Great Plains. My dad was a wheat farmer, and a national champion old-time fiddler," she says.

Yvonne's grandmothers quilted and wrote poetry, so perhaps that's where her two passions come from. "I am a traditional hand quilter," she says. "I have a collection of five generations of family quilts, all made on the prairies of the Northern Plains, some of them made in sod houses! I constantly work on quilts. I always have one in the frame and try to quilt a little every day (that I am home, that is), and always have a little packet of pieces to travel with. I have made many blocks while waiting for a doctor's appointment, sitting in an airport, and even on the airplane."

Yvonne is married to a lifelong cowboy/cattle rancher. Most of her poetry is about her life on the ranch or as a cowboy's wife, and quite a bit is humorous about situations that were not humorous when they happened.

She adds, a little shyly, "I am the top award-winning cowboy poet in America and, according to various sources, the top seller of books and CDs, as well as the most published by a cowgirl poet."

The Christmas Quilt

The first time that I saw it I was probably five years old.
 In fact, I don't remember it, but that's what I've been told.
My grandma started piecing it sometime 'fore I was born,
 and always got it out to show us all on Christmas morn.

You might call it a tradition just within our family;
 each year she'd take it from the trunk for all of us to see.
She'd tell us 'bout each little star that centered every block,
 and how she sewed 'em all together to form the pretty top.

She told us that the first block was made one winter night
 while thinking 'bout her sailor-boy . . . her heart was filled with fright.
'Twas late on Christmas Eve . . . she was lonely as could be;
 he was halfway 'round the world on a ship on a foreign sea.

Then thoughts came of another boy that was born that very night;
 and pointing to his birthplace was a great star shining bright.
He was born there in a stable to save us all from sin;
 she prayed he'd bless her sailor-son and please watch over him.

She took a scrap of fabric from her boy's favorite shirt
 and cut a star-shaped pattern, and then she went to work.
She made the first of many blocks that very Christmas Eve;
 it gave her peace to sew the stars from scraps of memories.

There were prints from mama's dresses and some from grandpa's clothes
 while others came from feed sacks she'd been saving, I suppose.
A little blue-checked star was from a tiny baby dress;
 it died so many years ago . . . her favorite I would guess.

Yvonne Hollenbeck

When she got the blocks completed she had made just forty-eight,
    the same as those upon the flag of our United States.
The hours she spent a-quilting it helped pass her time alone
    while waiting for her sailor-son to make it safely home.

She put a label on the back and packed the quilt away;
    she'd give it to her fine young lad when he returned one day.
The label said: "This Quilt was made for Christmas '41;
    'twas made with love to let you know I'm proud you are my son."

Then came the tragic message that her son would not come back;
    his ship was at the harbor when the Japanese attacked.
The quilt was left in her old trunk, along with several more,
    a folded flag, a Purple Heart, and clippings of the war.

It was exactly ten years later, Christmas morning, '51,
    the first time that she showed us all the quilt she'd made her son.
She told us all the story about each and every block
    she'd stitched a lot of memories there in every piece of cloth.

Now, many years have come and gone and Grandma's with her son,
    my granddad, and her baby; her life on earth is done.
I think of that first Christmas and that gift for you and me,
    and like so many soldier boys, Christ died to set us free.

I think of those who died for us and rest beneath the sod
    so we can live in freedom in one nation, under God
and forgetting all those sacrifices sometimes brings me guilt
    but I always am reminded when I see her Christmas Quilt.

The Cowboy and the Quilter

Did she know the consequences
when she became his wife,
or was she just enthralled
with exciting cowboy life?

She had watched a hundred movies
of Roy and Dale and Gene
and to be a cowboy's sweetheart
was beyond her wildest dreams.

So when she met a cowboy
with his horses and his ranch
she knew at once she was in love
and quick to take a chance.

But what those movies don't portray
and what she did not know
was all the chores she'd have to do
in sun and rain and snow;

the men she'd have to cook for;
the smelly laundry piles;
the orphan calves she'd have to nurse;
no neighbor gals for miles.

They claim she went to pieces
since she moved on his range.
Now, I won't say she's crazy,
but she is a little strange.

After all she buys good fabric
then she cuts it all apart,
then sews it back together,
which proves she's none too smart.

But the boys in the bunkhouse
have nice quilts on all their beds,
and in lieu of woolen saddle pads
there's patchwork ones instead.

They make a happy couple
and he doesn't seem to mind
that the sink is full of dishes
and the housework's way behind.

Although the ranch is quite neglected
neither seems to harbor guilt,
as he rides the range on his ol' horse,
she just sits and pieces quilts.

Yvonne Hollenbeck

Prairie Patchwork

There's a faded, handmade quilt on the sofa in her room,
and she always had it neatly folded there;
and when I'd ask about it, a smile came on her face;
it pleased her so to think that I would care.

She'd open it and tell about the making of each block,
and each one had a story of its own.
It was made when she was young and was living on the ranch
in a sod house that she called her "prairie home."

It was made from scraps of fabric from feed sacks she had saved,
or from worn-out clothes her children had outgrown;
and every single block in that pretty patchwork quilt
just seemed to fit together like a poem.

The pink block was the color of the early morning dawn,
and that crimson one like sumac in the fall;
yellow was the color of her roses by the gate,
and lilac was her favorite one of all.

The dark one made her think about those dry Depression years
when all the hills were parched and dirty brown.
Gray was like the rain that fell the day her husband died,
it was after that she had to move to town.

She said that life itself is like a patchwork quilt,
of births and deaths and all things in between;
and just when you are thinking that everything is fine,
along comes something new and unforeseen.

Just like her personal diary, as if she'd written in a book,
with the dawning and the passing of each year;
it seems her hopes and sorrows were recorded in each stitch
and each time that I read it brought a tear.

The story of her life, she said, was stitched in that old quilt;
on a corner on the back she signed her name;
then called it "Prairie Patchwork" . . . she wrote that on there too,
as a tribute to her life there on the plain.

Yvonne Hollenbeck

STACY JENNE

Douglas, Wyoming

Occasionally I get to do something for someone else. To "pay it forward," if you will. Stacy Jenne sent her two poems to me on the recommendation of another poet, who said, "I'm taking the liberty to recommend my ranch woman friend, Stacy, in case you'd be interested. I feel sure she'd be happy to send you some poems. She's relatively unpublished . . . puts out little books on her own and sells them to her friends, but I feel she has talent far beyond that, and lots of humor. She's also a paramedic, and was widowed when her husband's hay truck wrecked. I can contact her and give her your contact information if you are at all interested in her poems. Thanks for taking time to check them out." I did.

What struck me right away was Stacy's honesty in her letter to me. Clearly, she is a "beginner," but I know what that feels like. I was a beginner once myself, and someone gave me a chance. I never forgot that. Her poems made me chuckle and smile, and isn't that what writing and poetry is all about? I admit it, she "spoke" to me in more than a few ways. She wrote, "I am submitting two poems for your consideration. Work has been heck lately and I have not had time to get any poems to you. Until now.

"I have lived and worked on a ranch my entire life but just started writing poems in 2007. I don't necessarily write to be published but just to get things down on paper that interest me. I have been a paramedic for twenty-one years, and also write about some of the things we see on the streets, good and bad. I have attempted to write several poetry books, but I am my own publisher and sometimes it does not go so well. I just wanted to say thank for your time and good luck with the book. I have a saying: 'I am a paramedic for the money, a poet for the sanity, and a rancher for the hell of it.' God bless this country for letting me be all of these things."

The Cabin

Up amongst the brushy pines,
Where the river snakes and winds,
There stands a cabin off the beaten path,
That looks as though it's seen the devil's wrath.
For a hundred years it stood strong,
Thru winters that were forever long.
It was a haven to keep someone warm,
It was a shelter from the storm.
As you hear the whispers on the wind,
History still lingers from within.
Was it a homesteader's cabin or a line shack?
Was it a cowboy's camp and place to hang his kack?
Did a family live here and now are gone?
Are they buried nearby or did they just move on?
Memories are now trapped in this rotting wood,
In the pine trees where a cabin once stood.

Stacy Jenne

Ranch Women

Ranch women wear all kinds of hats,
Which one she wears depends on where she's at.
These ladies are wives, mothers and cooks,
They are the crappy-coverall-wearing cowgirls with good looks.
They are the riders, ropers and wild cow chasers across the plains,
They are the heifer-checking cow feeders in the snow and rain.
They are the truck fixers, bull haulers and cow milkers at midnight,
They are the up before dawn and ones finishing chores late into the night.
They are the horse wranglers, four-wheeler riders and irrigators,
They are the keepers of the peace and the cowboy de-escalators.
They are the bill payers and the keeper-of-the-ranch ladies,
They are the mow the yard so her cowboy can relax someplace shady.
They are the riders of the outside and don't forget to check the fence,
They are the talk to the bankers and make it make sense.
They are the gate wrestlers when the top wire is as tight as banjo string,
They are lip balm and nails done for a little bling.
They are the go to town for parts and hurry up, where's lunch,
They are the rush back home and help gather the big bunch.
They are the loaders of feed into the pickup and square bale tossers,
They are the cowboy wrangler cleaners and dirty dish washers.
They are the chicken feeders, calf bottlers and bovine vets,
They are as honest as the day is long and as good as it gets.
They are the calf wrestlers, vaccine givers and snack getters,
They are the do what needs to be done and never, ever, sitters.
The ranch women are the backbone of this Western range,
And let's hope for the sake of the cowboy this will never change!

DEE "BUCKSHOT DOT" STRICKLAND JOHNSON

Payson, Arizona

Dee Strickland Johnson (also known as "Buckshot Dot" or just plain "Dot") describes herself as a "female cowboy poet, author and artist, and hysterical relic." She's published five recordings of favorite Western classics and original songs and poems, and several books featuring original poems, songs, and artwork. "Buckshot Dot" is a favorite at cowboy poetry gatherings, and performs professionally at events and festivals "just for the love of it!" she laughs. She celebrates the "Old West" way of life with traditional cowboy songs and original poems, and she tells it "like it was."

Dot is an Arizona Culture Keeper. She has been the opening act for Lyle Lovett, was the Academy of Western Artists' Female Cowboy Poet of the Year in 1997, and has won numerous other awards and accolades. She has appeared in sixteen states, Canada, and the British Isles.

There is a gentle side to Dee. Her poem "Fredonia" has been described by fellow poet Virginia Bennett as "simply the most beautiful poem about a horse ever written." I have to agree with Virginia's praise.

Dot lives in Arizona with her husband, John.

Fredonia

I saddle up one afternoon
and happily I hum the tune
of some old plaintive cowboy song.
As if to say I got it wrong,
Fredonia shakes her mane and head,
and I believe she's firmly said,
"Cut the horse play; let's get on
the timber trail.
Forget the song."

The trail leads upward, twisting rising
toward the west where with surprising
artistry the sun in leaving
shafts of light will soon be weaving:
purple, gold and crimson bright
with empathizing shades of night.
A tremor threads Fredonia's spine
and somehow is transferred to mine.

Among the white-barked aspen trees
I touch the reins and press my knees
against her side. Fredonia halts
and turns to see if she's at fault.
I dismount to lie among
the fallen leaves, once green and young,
now crisp and curling, old and brown,
they cushion me
as I lie down.

Fredonia flicks her tail to say,
"Get up! We must be on the way!"
Refreshing dampness holds me, still
Fredonia's eyes are on the hills.
Reluctantly, I rise and straddle
the smooth cool leather of my saddle,
then reach to stroke the little mare
who really thinks
we're bound somewhere.

Legacy of Levi's

My Daddy swears by Levi's,
He says nothing else compares
To garments made by Levi Strauss;
    Of that we're all aware!

For if I'm wearin' Wrangler's
    or Lees, he looks askance,
"You can call 'em jeans if you want to;
Sure as hell ain't cowboy pants!"

So, of course, I'm wearin' Levi's—
It's in the "genes," you see,
And I'll tell you the tale of Levi's
Just as it was told to me:
How an immigrant started his fortune
Back in 1853:

Strauss came to California
    With tough brown canvas meant for tents
    To house the myriad miners
    Who had emigrated west
To the siren call of gold fields;
    But the mother lode had waned,
    by the time young Levi got there.
An old prospector explained:

"Son, a lot of folks has left here
    There's tents available galore.
You should have brought good britches—
    Them's the thing we're needin' more!"

Dee "Buckshot Dot" Strickland Johnson

Levi listened to the miners:
     "For the gold we hope to pack,
We need tight gold-dust-proof pockets,
     Also pockets in the back,
Sturdy seams with reinforcement."
     Levi thought he'd take a chance,
Cut his canvas into pieces
     And he started making pants.

"Closer fit for work in water."
     Levi set about to please.
Took his pattern from the sailor
     pants worn by the Genoise:
Therefore, known as "jeans" thereafter,
(Which Strauss didn't want them called.
He persisted in insisting
     They are waist-high overalls").

First he used his tough brown canvas;
Then he tried out something new:
Making pants from firm French cotton
     dyed with indigo—deep blue.
Serge de Nimes—or simply "denim"—
Which soon proved that it would do.

Came along then Jacob Davis,
Still another immigrant;
He'd set rivets on horse blankets,
Offered them for Levi's pants.
They added belt loops, orange thread,

And this leather patch here on the rear,
And Levi Strauss became the foremost
Of the trousers worn out here
    in the west among the miners
And the men who followed near
To provide them beef and cowhides
On the west's great last frontier.

Now there used to be a rivet
At the bottom of the fly;
But that's been discontinued,
And here's the reason why:
The cowboy was responsible,
For quite often he would squat
Beside the roaring campfire—
And that rivet sure got hot!
(That's why that one has been removed
From that strategic spot.)

That's the cowboy's contribution
    to these pants he calls his own.
Why, they're tough as saddle leather.
And they wear just like a stone!
So my Daddy's plumb convinced me—
This not some passing fad
And that's how I came to treasure
    the best pants Man ever had!
It's the Legacy of Levi's—
And I got it from my Dad.

Dee "Buckshot Dot" Strickland Johnson

Rawhide Annie

We called her Rawhide Annie,
She was big and bad and tough,
Except when she was drinkin'—
Then she didn't seem so rough.

She owned a ranch out west of town,
Run a hundred head or more;
And no one crossed old Annie,
For she packed a forty-four!

She could rope and ride and lie and cuss
The way all cowhands can.
In her Levi's, boots, and grubby hat
She looked just like a man.

She came to town one Friday night
And stopped for a few stiff shots,
Till the barkeep called, "Five minutes, gents,
Five more is all you've got!"

We hangers-on all tossed 'em down
And were puttin' on our coats
When, from the far end of the bar,
Annie loudly cleared her throat.

She announced while peepin' in her hands
That she'd formed in a kind of dome,
"The guy that names what's in my hands,
Will get to take me home!"

A loud guffaw. A wry voice cried,
"A big bad longhorn steer!"
"Whoa!" said Ann, peepin' in her hands,
"We got a winner here!"

RANDI JOHNSON

Great Basin, Oregon

Randi Johnson describes herself as "a Great Basin buckaroo and rodeo queen." She grew up on ranches in Nevada, California, and eastern Oregon, and has a passion for promoting the agriculture industry and the sport of rodeo. She proudly carries on buckaroo traditions in her dress and manner, which also helps to make her a standout in rodeo parades, with her flat hat and tapaderas (covered leather stirrups), riding her pinto ranch horse.

"Being raised in this lifestyle has given me a wealth of experiences," she says with a smile. "The old cowboy's stories, along with my love of history, are what I draw on when I write." It should be noted she has been writing poetry since she was fourteen years old, and has filled many journals. I have had the pleasure of hearing her poetry several times, and it always "rings true."

Mary Williams Hyde, a noted photographer of ranch gatherings in the Great Basin of Oregon and Nevada, where the buckaroos rope and ride, had this to say about her "nominated" poet, Randi Johnson. "Randi is a beautiful young woman shaped by a lifetime of exposure to the best of traditional buckaroo-style horsemanship and stockmanship. I have been photographing her, as well as her family, since 2006.

"For a girl educated by homeschooling (and doing her college work now), the quality of Randi's work is a nice surprise. She is a naturally skilled communicator and a wordsmith with rare talent. I look forward to seeing how life unfolds for her as a young woman."

Silent Stories

Old barn I long to hear your stories, sometimes I see them in my dreams,
The hard work and histories, shadowed by your graying eaves,
Old stone foundation almost reclaimed by the brush,
With old pumps and pencil tins all gone back to rust,
In the middle of the desert, no water in sight,
Did your 'steaders slowly starve out, or leave overnight?
Rock wall fence and wooden swinging gate,
I want to know your craftsman, but I am decades too late,
Dugout caves with traces of burnt-out fires,
Snake-oil bottles under abandoned telephone wires,
Skeletons of a past hardscrabble society,
Traces kicked over by my horse's feet,
Oil lamp bases, barely readable coffee cans,
Rusted Model A fenders, buckshot frying pans,
History that the sagebrush overgrows,
Stories that no one anymore knows,
I want to hear your legends, tall tales, and lies,
Your groans of pain and widow's cries,
What secrets are you keeping under your desert sands,
Tales of hard work and calloused hands,
Rock houses shadowed by cottonwood trees,
Carved initials and brands under autumn leaves,
Memories taken to unmarked graves,
Roads almost invisible, well-traveled but never paved,
Ghost towns and mine shafts under skies of blue,

Explored only by pack-rats and curious buckaroos,
Mysteries I may never figure out,
Because the tellers of your stories are fading out,
But I will dream of your era when I sleep tonight,
'Cause ghost towns are in my blood, my forefathers fought your fight.

Randi Johnson

Advice

It's sometimes funny the advice us ranch girls get,
Always act like a lady but still watch where you spit,
It's okay to work like a man in your Daddy's old shirt,
But always keep on hand high heels and a lacy skirt,
All sunshine makes a desert,
Don't bank on the weather,
Trust your neighbor but brand your cattle,
Don't bring a knife into a gun battle,
There is a difference between a cowboy and a cattleman,
And he is neither if he won't shake your hand,
You shouldn't ask a man the size of his spread,
But you have a right to know if you're going to be wed,
Keep your mind in the middle and your forked end down,
And dress to kill when you dress for town,
No horse can run faster than you can ride,
Let someone know when you take a young horse outside,
Always be aware of what is around you,
Some of the best riding is done when the skies aren't blue,
One of the quips that influenced me the most,
I heard when I was fifteen or so,
Paint your toenails so when you're sleeping in desert sand,
When you pull your socks on you remember that you're still a woman,
But there is one that surpassed them all I think,
It was Brian Neubert who told me, "Just don't go marryin' a dink."

Dusty Desert Roads

I'm going out into this world, leaving behind all I've known,
As I step into this city, I find myself missing my dusty desert roads,
Where men are measured by what they do, not the titles of their names,
Where 4-H Notes in the paper are the equivalent of fame,
Where you can stay out all night with friends and family,
Where you never hear the words "I'm just too busy,"
Where guns and trucks and horses are a part of daily life,
Where women help their husbands, proud to be a cowboy's wife,
You can drive all across the countryside and hit the pavement twice,
The only time you drive between the lines is on the way home Friday night,
The UPS man drives a minivan to your front gate,
Then leaves the package on the ground before the cowdogs wake,
Where kids go to school in a one-room class,
K thru eight all together and all five of them pass,
Socialization comes at branding time and rodeos,
Life is sweet and simple down these dusty desert roads,
Loose haystacks and almost worn-out Wranglers,
Where it isn't odd for friends to date each other's sisters,
Sewing, canning, and braiding are all still thriving arts,
Church is miles away but we worship in our hearts,
Dust clouds rise and drift across the flats,
Jackrabbits and cattle crisscross tire tracks,
Little boys run traplines all thru the winter months,
Then help their dads make hay when the school year is up,
I'm turning back towards the desert, in town I don't belong,
I'm going back to where Aldean fades into old country songs,
Where daddies only get in late after fixing trailer lights,
Where you cannot hear the highway for the coyotes at night,

Randi Johnson

Where neighbors know each other by their first names,
Where parents drive for hours to watch the home games,
So when the time has come and I have packed my last load,
Just go ahead and park me at the end of a dusty desert road.

Who Were They

As I sit on this fence and wonder,
I wish to see the young you,
When your posts were fresh hewn,
What bronc rides did you see,
What stories did you hear,
Who stained your planks,
With tobacco, blood, and tear,
Who sat on these planks where I sit now,
Who branded calves, who milked a cow,
Back when this tall grass was cropped short,
Who rode the horses, who made the sort,
Old broken-down corrals like this,
In every corner of the basin,
I wish you could tell me, who were they?
And what dreams were they chasin'?

JO LYNNE KIRKWOOD

Sigurd, Utah

With a wide, Western smile, Jo Lynne Kirkwood launches right into telling about herself. "I've been involved with farming and ranching all my life," she says. Her family came from rural northern Arizona, where they raised cattle and hay on land that had always been in her family. She lives with her husband, Michael, in central Utah, where they raise grass and alfalfa, as well as livestock. Jo Lynne is a writer and an artist. She teaches writing and fine arts. "Michael and I have designed and, for the past five years, have been building our own home. This is an entirely creative process!" she laughs.

She writes about the people she knows, or has known, and about real events from her life. "Much of what I write is humorous," she says, "because life is often funny—especially in retrospect." Jo Lynne has been writing and performing rhymed narrative stories for over twenty years, and has won several awards. She has been named Female Poet of the Year by the Academy of Western Artists in 2009, has been a Lariat Laureate on Cowboypoetry.com, has gathered up several "first place" prizes in contests, and has been published in various magazines and other places. She is frequently invited to festivals and gatherings, or to entertain for other events.

Indoor Plumbing

Grandma had it pretty hard, living far from town and friends
She canned most of the food they ate, sewed quilts from odds and ends,
But the conditions she complained of most, when cold winds made her shiver
Were the trips out to the outhouse, and that board seat full of slivers.

So Grandpa installed plumbing. It was a big surprise.
Took out the dry sink and the icebox, left a space just the right size

For a privy and a basin. Then he hung a curtain on a rod
For privacy there in the kitchen. Although it seemed a little odd

Whenever someone took a rest you could recognize their feet
On the floor beneath the curtain, while they were sitting on the seat.
Grandpa sent Gran off to Ada's so she wouldn't know what's
While he pulverized her dry sink and removed her old icebox.

They had the rural electric; the icebox should have been replaced
But the refrigerator that Gramps hauled in took three times the space.
It would not fit in the kitchen so it leaned against the wall
Like an obese metal snowman, by the door in the front hall.

Grandma had to have a sink, to wash the plates and cups
But when the commode replaced the dry sink, the space was all filled up
So Grandpa ran a waterline into the living room.
He built a sink and some new cupboards, with slot for Grandma's broom.

Then outside, beside the front door, opposite the sink,
he attached a porcelain urinal, so the dog could get a drink.
And with plumbing in the living room, the logical next move
Was to add an indoor bathtub. He knew Grandma would approve

Because it was such a chore to haul in water then heat it up 'til hot
And they both took baths each Saturday, whether they needed them or not.
In the war Grandpa had been to France, and he knew some Frenchie ways
So he thought he ought to spoil Grandma, and he bought a French bidet

But Grandma, when she got back home, saw no need for it
Said unless he put it in the yard, it probably wouldn't fit

So Gramps left it there in the front yard. And folks would get a laugh
Because from April clear through summer it made a fine birdbath.

Now Grandma was quite fussy. She cleaned and polished every day
And some ladies might have been upset to have their homes arranged that way
But Grandma, she just grinned and smiled, stayed quiet as a mouse
Because she was so dang tickled to have plumbing installed all through the house.

Jo Lynne Kirkwood

Gina

Gina lived in a two-room shack at the edge of an empty field.
Her father worked on the Big Navajo at the Whiting Brothers' sawmill.
The wooden slats that formed her floor were rough-sawn, gnarled and wide,
And autumn winds blew through the gaps and chilled the house inside.

Coins and dust and buttons fell through those rough-hewn boards,
We'd crawl beneath the cabin and find treasures we would hoard.
We kept our riches in a cocoa can in a secret hiding place,
A rainbow sprinkle of tiny beads, a penny with an Indian face.

The Kaibab mill paid poor man's wages to all the reservation men
Who'd come to town with their wives and children then soon go home again.
Sometimes they came for a few weeks only, sometimes two months or more,
But Gina's family called the town their home. That cabin with the drafty floor.

Elastic bands and checkers, a ring without a stone
A photograph of a soldier someone, sometime, had known
Valentines and bottle caps, a single tinted lens
Bubblegum comics and bobby pins, precious things we found back then.

Gina came to school so scrubbed and clean no one could ever know
about the little shack with the floorboard cracks or the Kaibab Big Navajo.
Daisy and Beth also came to school. Reservation Indian kids,
who lived somewhere between the desert and town, just like Gina did.

Glossy braids hung down their backs as thick as heavy ropes.
They would not look at the teacher. Bowed their heads when the teacher spoke.
When the traveling nurse from Flagstaff came to make her monthly rounds
she cut off their braids with shining shears. They fell upon the ground.

No one asked her reasons, though her actions seemed so cold.
The Indian kids spread head lice. Or so we had been told.
Gina's eyes were dark and clear but that day they lost their glow.
She didn't say a single word, just took her seat, her head bent low.

Baseball cards and hair barrettes, a name tag without a name,
Barbershop wooden nickels, a Doublemint wrapper chain.
A ragged old lace hanky that was falling all apart,
The tab from a broken zipper, a faded queen of hearts.

The next day when Gina came to school her hair was bobbed and curled.
Ribbons were tied above each ear, like all the other girls.
But Daisy and Beth never returned again that year to school.
They went back home to the reservation where people weren't so cruel.

Jo Lynne Kirkwood

Quilting Party

On porches, in churches, or community halls, in towns with a thousand names,
Tables are pushed back to the walls to make room for the rails and frames,
And women gather, as they have done since the first settlers arrived
On small farmsteads, networked by wagon rut roads, linking the lands and lives

Of women whose days were marked by toil. Skin chilblained and scarred,
Faces coarsened and lined by the wind. Lives dreary and hard.
Yet still they would gather. If need be in barns, or in the shade on a cottonwood knoll
To comfort, encourage, together create these gifts from the feminine soul.

Pinwheels, Log Cabins, Friendship Gardens, Tulips, a Crown of Thorns,
Tiny squares clipped from the hem of a skirt where the fabric was less worn.
Hawks, Jacob's Ladders, Lovers Quarrel Knots, Flower Baskets, a Wild Goose Chase,
Listen. You'll hear voices in each faded block from a long ago time and place.

Dorie is copying an old Danish pattern from a quilt her great-grandmother carried
Wrapped 'round her wedding dress, tucked in a trunk across the long lonely prairie.
And Inez is binding the edges. She says she'll show us a stitch
She remembers from her Aunt Floris, who passed on in '86.

"Too bad you young girls didn't know her," she says, though we're most over forty.
"She knew all there was about stitching, I guess. Good to have her at a quilting party."
Nana's unknotting a long piece of thread, and looks up with a laugh and a smile.
"But now we've got you," she says, gentle-voiced. "Just be sure you stay here awhile."

Victory Stars, Maypoles, Old Maid's Puzzle Boxes, Honeycombs, Fans, Irish Lace,
Treasures fashioned from cuttings and scraps, stored away in an old pillowcase.
Moonbeams and Sunbursts, Long Country Roads, Stairsteps, Daniel Boone's Frying Pan,
Testaments to the tenacious spirits of the women who settled this land.

And here, even now, women gather. As they long have, and as they will again,
To remember, rejoice, share sorrow and laughter, and to work, as they do, with their hands.
They will sort out the news of their families, talk of friends who've moved far away,
Discuss recipes, patterns, the worries and joy of the lives that they live day to day

As they appliqué, baste, and embroider, blanket-stitch, gather and seam
Heirlooms for new generations made of fabric and memories, and dreams.
Grandmothers, aunts, daughters and nieces, neighbor gals, mothers and wives,
Carefully stitching the remnants and pieces. The crazy quilts of all our lives.

Jo Lynne Kirkwood

ECHO KLAPROTH

Shoshoni, Wyoming

Echo Klaproth is a fourth-generation Wyoming rancher who began writing to pay tribute to the unique heritage her family has enjoyed since 1876, raising livestock on ground homesteaded by their great-grandparents in northeast Wyoming.

Over the years, she's published chapbooks, "fine lines" from twenty years of cowboy poetry gatherings, and produced a CD of original and classic poetry. Her latest work, *Words Turn Silhouette*, is a memoir and study of the many and varied cycles of women's lives.

One of Echo's proudest accomplishments came in 1995, when she was invited to participate in a live ranch radio program at the Smithsonian in Washington, D.C. It's a teaching point she uses to encourage writers. "Keep it real, write with integrity, and never give up," she says, "because you don't know where a few words might take you."

Echo and her husband, Rick, live on a small farm near Shoshoni, Wyoming. After retiring from teaching, she was ordained a minister and became the chaplain with a nonprofit hospice organization. This Wyoming poet and writer has written songs, a newspaper column, started a novel, and always has a journal going.

Echo was named Wyoming's sixth Poet Laureate. She believes poetry has served as the impetus to get her to the place God intended for her all along—to serve Him by encouraging others in their walks in life with words both written and spoken.

The God Whisperer

Two thousand years have come and gone
for the feminine of men
and with manes and tails a'flowing
we're like mares loose in the pen:
palomino and blue-eyed roan,
black, gray and buckskin hues,
thoroughbreds and quarter horses,
ponies and Percheron too.

Some mill around like colts unsure,
skittish and likely to bolt,
while others stand hip-locked, asleep;
unlikely they'll revolt.
Some pay attention with heads up
alert while ears catch all,
but others plug along, heads down,
nowhere in their wherewithal.

It's the haughty, those sure-footed,
who are hardest to control;
'cause without sense we charge the gate,
stir the herd with rigmarole.
The unsure, we stand shivering,
unkind voices nudging in;
there's a nervous bit of tension
when the whispering begins.

Though some began life with His words
we've forgotten most of them,
so He gently breathes into us
what we need to know again.
He's the patience in impatience,
love and truth are His whips;
and if we turn our hearts around,
it's with passion He'll equip.

He examines the pen of us,
watchful eye on problem signs,
then with loving intuition,
He reads between the lines—
unwearyingly waits on buckers,
disregards transgression's due,
ignores the proud and stubborn ones,
absolves those faithful few.

He disdains the use of anger
but He'll use it if He must,
as He whispers out instructions
with His all-enduring trust.
Then He sorts through His remuda
for the ones he'll use this day
and He turns us out to carry
the Message on our way.

Echo Klaproth

In Her Mind

In her mind he's out a fencin'
or doin' chores around,
and he'll be in for dinner soon—
but only in her mind.

She stands and stares out the glass
from the home where she's been placed,
and ev'ry car's a horse and rider—
but only in her mind.

She's at the ranch, her family's here,
of this there is no doubt,
'cause she can see and hear them clear—
but only in her mind.

Her children play, the garden's growin'
and things are just the same;
she still bakes bread and works all day—
but only in her mind.

Flowers grow beneath the line
she planted there with care,
beside the house so tall and proud—
but only in her mind.

They moved her in a year ago,
she didn't cope with change;
nothing aged or ever died—
but only in her mind.

No, she doesn't feel the close confines
because she's at the ranch
with mem'ries strong and all intact—
but only in her mind.

A Ride Across the Pasture

As I ride across the pasture golden,
engulfed in scent—bouquet of sage and hay—
I find my mind easily goes wandering
picturing how it was on an earlier day.

It's hard to imagine this land I know
without progress and its consequences.
God, I bet it was grand, topping a rise,
seeing uncluttered miles with no fences.

I've heard the grass used to be some taller
and water ran clear in our now dry creek;
you could ride for miles without a stop and,
except by chance, not see neighbors for a week.

I'm sure the sounds were more comforting:
a breeze whispering by or the cows a'bawling,
instead of a truck roaring away
or a pumpjack up the draw a'squalling.

While knowing I'm luckier than others
there's an awareness—I'm sadder than most,
because I'm riding across this pasture
looking for a picture forever lost.

Echo Klaproth

DEANNA DICKINSON McCALL

Timberon, New Mexico

Deanna Dickinson McCall has cows, horses, and a love of the land bred into her. She comes from a family that began ranching in Texas in the 1840s. She has ranched in several Western states, including twenty-two years raising her family on a remote Nevada ranch without phones or electricity.

The woman who nominated her for inclusion in this book, Therese Taylor Staeger, was born into ranching on the Wind River Reservation at Lander, Wyoming, in 1935. She says, "I am a great admirer of Deanna Dickinson McCall . . . Deanna's stories and poems tell the real story of ranching—the hardships, joys, and bad times. She has lived through it and survived to work another day at what she loves. This is who she is . . . It is her life. It is a hard life but a good life, like no other. Ranchers are a tight-knit group of people who are there for one another in times of need. Deanna's poem 'Cow Country Code' pretty well sums it up."

Deanna performs her poetry throughout the West at gatherings from the National Cowboy Poetry Gathering in Elko, Nevada, to the Texas Cowboy Poets Gathering in Alpine, Texas. Her book *Mustang Spring: Stories & Poems* was published by the Frontier Project and has been nominated for several awards, as well as winning the WMA Poetry Book of the Year award in 2014. Deanna's poetry CD, *Riding*, was selected as Album of the Year for 2012 by the Academy of Western Artists, and her poem "Cow Country Code" won the Georgie Sicking Award for 2014. Her poems and stories are included in several anthologies. She is currently working on her next book. She and her husband ranch in the Sacramento Mountains of southern New Mexico.

Cow Country Code

I listened carefully, listened to directions
All based on recollections
Of cattle last seen, water and grass green.

His face was lined, lined from a lifetime
Of counting every nickel and dime
Worries and cares, hopes and prayers.

He'd outlived his child, outlived his wife
Seemed to have tired of life
After the stroke, spirit and body broke.

Drought had fallen, fallen heavy on the land
Grass replaced by piles of sand
Tanks lay long dry, under a blazing sky.

We prowled around, prowled for his cows
Swore to ourselves renewed vows
Of helping neighbors, and our free labor.

But, we faced mortality, faced our own years
And sought to appease our fears
Of growing old, and outfits sold.

Cattle were gathered, gathered and sorted
Numbers tallied and reported
We figured the amount, he was given the count.

Deanna Dickinson McCall

It would be enough, would buy a place in town
To watch the sun go down
On a quiet street, with memories bittersweet.

His old hand shook, shook as the paper curled
That gave a dollar amount to his world
He took our word, couldn't really see the herd.

That tally he held, held with quiet pride
Was one time we all lied
We'd padded the count, added to the amount.

His cattle were thin, were rough and open
Hadn't calved like we were hopin'
We added a few, ours, and he never knew.

It was our raising, raised to do right
In the old days of black and white
No question of gray, only one right way.

We rode hard, hard and long all day
For something more valued than pay
A time-honored code, for this we rode.

He & I

We rode thru brush laden with thorn and berry
Under showers of green needles and cones
On narrow ridges we rode carefully and wary
Circling boulders, sliding on loose stone.

We rode through the gilded world of Fall
Where squirrels scampered with foodstuff
While bull elk bugled their chilling call
From a mountainside steep and rough.

We rode for the first gather, he and I
Watching for cattle hiding in brush
The silent ones that let you ride by
Others exploding like quail we flushed.

We rode on a golden day of early Autumn
When the snakes stretch out and sleep
Trailing Corriente cows to the bottom
Through mountains high, canyons deep.

We rode in silence while nature spoke
In tongues of breeze, wing and cry
And the snap of twigs critters broke
Spoke of silent watchers nearby.

We rode for the first gather of the Fall, he and I
In apple-crisp air heady as red wine
Trailing cattle while the earth sighed
At cows and riders in golden sunshine.

Deanna Dickinson McCall

The Good Years

The soft sound of hooves on leaves
Shuffling over rock on the slope,
The gentle pull uphill as you look
Praying for grass, praying for hope.

It's autumn and no rain has fallen
No summer monsoons ever came.
Last year's grass is gone to dust
Too many years of the same.

You recall waving grama grass
Cured brown with seed on the stem
It would put a cow through winter
Up here on the ridge and rim.

But, it rained at least some,
Even those marginal years had grass
The springs and creeks flowed
Laden clouds didn't blow past.

You relive the really good years
The land was unbelievably green
You rode in mud fixing water gaps
Tanks blown, canyons scoured clean.

Grass and wildflowers was stuff of fairies
Seeds and blooms nodding to dancing dew
Cows and horses sleek and shiny fat
Lord, it was like the land was new.

Those memories keep you hanging on,
Heaven-sent rains would finally come.
You have been in tight spots before
Tough old times, you've seen some.

Drier than the dirty thirties
Record dry they say.
God will open the heavens
Wash this drought clean away.

'Til then, you pull your hat down
Squint through the dust some more
Summon faith back in your heart
That God will heal this land's sore.

Close your tired eyes against the dust
See the fat cattle and green grass
Feel the moisture on the soft wind
Dream of the good years of the past.

RENEE MEADOR

Big Horn, Wyoming

Renee is a retired secondary mathematics teacher, fortunate enough to be living in the county where she was raised, Sheridan County, Wyoming. In her forty-plus years in education, she taught and lived in Texas and Ohio, as well as Wyoming. "I learned early in my own education the importance of being able to express myself in writing," she states.

An introduction to horses at an early age sparked a lifelong interest and love. By the time she was raising her own family, horses and Angora goats had joined the menagerie of 4-H animals.

"As a writer, I have progressed from prose published in *Buckeye Farm News* and the Ohio statewide newspaper *Farm and Dairy* to primarily memoir and poetry," she explains. "Topics include ranching and riding, narrative poems of Western events and people, poems about Western flora and fauna, as well as nature in general. I write poetry that seeks to reveal the attitudes and sentiments, experiences and journeys that molded the West and its people."

This writer of prose and poetry has two grown children and seven grandchildren, but she is quick to point out, "I enjoy being outdoors, in the mountains as much as possible, preferably on a horse! While horseback, I have a sense of how life used to be and am compelled to memorialize those who came before me by telling their stories, stories of how the West was and how their legacy continues today."

Nevada Mustang, Wyoming Autumn

Sabrina quit herding the gray mare
to move toward me
so when she stopped
I closed the gap.

We stand huddled together
in autumn predawn chill
as I stroke her roan-dappled
winter coat, warm and soft as Angora mittens.

Her neat, unshod black hooves,
beside my barn boots,
bespeak her inheritance
from hard-hoofed, mustang stock
running free for generations,
dependent on their instinct,
their intelligence, and their feet,
where lameness equals vulnerability.

We dream together as stars fade;
I, of cherished summer days
when she safely carried me
wherever I asked her to go,
believing in me more than
I believed in myself.

Sabrina? Perhaps her dream
is of decades past
predawn fall mornings,
with winter in the air
of the great Southwest,
sparse feed, distant water,
full moon setting. Venus rising.

Renee Meador

This Place: Red-Tailed Hawk over Two-Penny Rock

I love this place.
I love the sun upon my face.
I love to hear the raucous cry
of raven black or hawk on high,
band of red, a flash of fire
riding thermals ever higher.
I love this place.

I love this place.
I love the solitude of space.
I love the wind so wild and free
that carelessly caresses me,
whirls aloft across the pine
whispering of things Divine.
I love this place.

February Respite

Five deer
under the pheasant tree
at dawn, two whitetailed does
with last spring's fawns,
seek what the pheasant seek
where bare ground breaks
through snow cover
this February thaw.

Washed in muted crimson
from the eastern sky,
they nibble cured grasses
ever cautious
of my neighbor's dogs
and the lone coyote
who crosses my road,
howls at the winter moon.

A Treat (haiku)

eight below zero
bay horse exhales sunlit puffs
drifting mini-clouds

LYN MESSERSMITH

Alliance, Nebraska

Lyn Messersmith is a third-generation rancher in Cherry County, Nebraska. She is also a newspaper columnist and freelance writer. She has earned her spurs and hung them up but, as she says, "I haven't sold my saddle or cows!" Lyn hangs her hat at the home ranch as well as at her husband's home place in Sheridan County, and lives part-time in her pickup, traveling with Deb Nolting to present writing workshops and historical programs for the Nebraska and South Dakota Humanities Councils. She doesn't much care what else you say about her as long as it's something her mother would have liked to hear. So I will say that her poetry rings true, with a sassy touch of humor in it. She is intimate with her place in the West, and I think her mother would be proud of her.

The Entertainers

We were short a few eggs for breakfast
'Cause a weasel got in with the hens.
I should have set the trap instead
Of sprinklers for the weanin' pens.

The corral's a mudhole this morning
I let the tank run over again.
Lingered too long in the kitchen
Gettin' supper for all those men.

I tied my mare in the back stall
Too short. Forgot she won't have that.
Got busted reins and headstall now.
What's worse, she stomped on my hat.

I tripped on a hunk of baler twine
That someone forgot to pick up,
Let two heifers out the wrong gate
'Cause I got mad and cussed out that pup.

She's in the way half the day;
Too timid, or eager the rest.
I know she just needs time to learn,
And like me, she's doin' her best.

Now we can't find the dehornin' saw.
Guess I put it away too well.
Proof that when you put Ma in charge
The day's gonna go straight to hell.

I offered to quit, and go to the house
But the boss man won't play that game.
Poor devils would have no fun at all
Without the old woman to blame.

So that pup and I talked it over.
We're really not all that abused.
Just doin' the job no one else wants,
And keepin' the cowboys amused.

The Bargain

I was leavin' the local Western store
When the owner called out my name.
"Do you like this color?" he queried.
I said, "Sure, I'm always fair game
For new duds and doodads to deck me out,
And that's 'bout my favorite hue."
"New line," he says, "Cut a new way.
Colors are softer; the fabric is too.
Better take this scarf for a test drive.
You're right, that shade flatters you."

"For free?" I ask with a sly little grin.
'Cause it's my custom to bargain some.
"Well . . . okay, I guess," came a faint reply,
But the look on Mike's face was sure glum.
Behind the counter, Jerolyn winked.
Said, "There's probably a poem in there."
"Right," I replied, and made my escape.
Didn't dream Mike would take on my dare.
I get a twinge of guilt, now and then,
But I stole that scarf fair and square!

Mike's sold me a saddle, a slew of jeans,
Jewelry, belts, boots, blankets, and tack.
He's got the only game in town too,
So it's certain I'm gonna be back.
Mike and I both got a bargain that day.

There's a secret to the sales clerk's wink.
This is one wild rag Mike couldn't move.
You'll agree, if you just stop and think.
No rough tough rancher just off the range
Would be caught dead in this shade of pink.

Out to Pasture

It can't be spring so soon. Oh surely not.
She's supposed to announce herself clearly
With crane calls slippin' silver down the wind
While I'm stretchin' wire on some sandy hill,
Or the sudden sound of a meadowlark's trill;
My mount's response to the press of a knee,
Layers of warmth on my winter white skin,
And pairs mothered up in the calving lot.

I know it's not spring. Look here, you see
My coveralls are clean. No streaks of black
From windmill grease, or wrenches, on my palm.
Still, season's edges blur, when markers disappear.
Things I used to know, in hindsight, aren't so clear.
'Causin' me to ponder if I've got the knack
For layin' down the reins without a qualm.
That notion's unnatural, for the likes of me.

Spring always arrives with dirt on her face
And hands. We hug, and it rubs off on mine.
A birthmark is transferred, deepened each year.
But now, no blood of birthing soils my sleeve.
At my window watch, I seem to perceive
That night horse tied by the barn as a sign
We're off duty now, and that's mighty queer
Since we still have our hearts in the race.

Green-up comes on in the pasture that waits
For him and me; outside the circle now.
I scoured these hands, rain baptized my clothes,
Soaked my soul in ninety proof, baked it in the sun.
Offered it to the moon, but really, what I've done
Was hock it cheap, to buy just one more cow.
Hoss, that springtime wind's sure bitter when it blows.
You check that grass, while I go close the gates.

She Speaks to Me

KATHY MOSS

Canyon City, Oregon

Kathy Moss, also known as A.K. Moss, is very definite about who she is. She states, "I am not a cowgirl. I am a Western woman." She lives in Grant County in eastern Oregon.

Like so many other Western women, Kathy is happy working, keeping up the home front, supporting the community, and living a Western life. Her stories and poetry reflect this. Her quiet voice, when she recites one of her poems, commands that you listen. Her sense of cadence and rhythm is excellent. I overheard someone say, after Kathy recited a poem to an appreciative audience, "I really liked that and I don't like poetry!"

Kathy's writing comes straight from the heart. She writes about what she knows and believes in. "I don't ask for a lot," she says. "Mainly support and understanding, quiet time in the horse corral, or just sitting and writing." She and her good friend Billie Price Flick (who told me about Kathy) can often be found horseback together, working cattle, breaking young horses, or just lolling along a trail, talking. Billie says of her friend of over ten years, "Kathy writes from the heart, her poetry is real, and she has lived it."

Kathy has been published in several different publications, including *The Big Roundup* and *Cascade Horseman*. Her CD, *Dear Charlie*, is a tribute in poetry to Charlie Russell and others who have influenced her.

Cowgirl

Her life a little rough, her spirit you couldn't tame,
Her heart running wild, Cowgirl is her name.
More than punchin' cattle and branding in the spring,
The fences need mending so wire she'd string.
The colts need startin', they need an honest hand,
By midsummer with confidence and trust they'd stand.
Haying season already started, swathed and ready to rake.
She is up and on the tractor before the sun begins to break.
Bucking bales in the heat of the day to take them to the stack,
Everyone pulls their own weight, no one's looking back.
Sorting pairs and pushing cattle, fall is setting in,
The days are getting shorter, and it's feeding time again.
Now calving season started, it's babies she'd tend,
The cold, weak, and poor, she would help them stand again.
When they are warmed, fed and on their feet again,
They are taken to their mommas to tell where they'd been.
No sooner one out the door, another takes its place,
Cold, wet, shivering, with pink nose and brock face.
Now spring is coming soon, the circle closing once again,
The same as it had done since time had begun.
The routine starts again, to start another year.
Branding is coming soon, to start it good and clear.
Though the years fade in and out and seasons come and go,
The work is never done, but the days she'll always know
She might question her life, and to what it has led,
But only for an hour or two, and just before bed,
And when in the morning the sun begins to rise
Her coffee in her hand, her soul has no lies.
She heads to the barn, her head held with pride,
The only way she will leave is when she takes her last ride.

Wink, Nod and Sigh

She has felt a rope with a mustang attached,
Threw berries into a biscuit batch,
The holes she'd patch in clothes and shoes
She loves her life and has paid her dues,
She has tallied and rallied, opened the gate,
Chased and paced and could hardly wait,
For true love to come calling and fulfill her life,
Yet the blue of her falling and the dreams of a wife
Would have to wait until there was more time in the day,
For her fate would not dawn on her or come her way
Until she gathered her emotions and set them aside,
'Til she lathered all horses she started to ride,
And found out that tough is not all that there is,
And what she's done comes back on her, the takes and the give.
She has gathered and sorted, she's worked dawn till dark,
She's been lathered and courted, jerked drawn and embarked,
Into places with horses she never thought existed,
Keeping paces through courses that she has enlisted.
She has draped and dallied, taped and cursed,
Coped and prodded, roped and worse,
She has caught things she didn't want to and tried to turn loose,
Been drug, whipped, and burned, yet learned to cook goose.
She has folded, molded, and tarried too long,
Charmed, harmed, and done things wrong,
Brought laughter where tears stain the face,
Taught love, soothed fears, she has attempted grace.
She has held many a child, colt and calf,
With the hands the size of man's, only half,
And the calluses that line them may dull the feel,
Yet her heart, it binds them to a mother so real.

Kathy Moss

She has procrastinated, assassinated, tallied and stewed,
Migrated, almost been abominated, is liberated and has brewed
Over family, friends, dinner and such,
All she has, all she wants, which isn't that much.
She has cursed God, loves the Bible and believes in Amen.
If she had her druthers she'd do it over again,
And the source of remorse behind her eyes,
With all her give up and failures that she tries to disguise,
Only haunts the face that in the mirror lies.
It taunts a trace in the lines of grace and gives her knowledge she can now recognize.
Then that moment is gone, she fixes her hair, with a hum of a song
that gently tickles the air,
The wind in her wake is the aftermath, for she has learned to walk another path
To keep her life whole, that is embedded deep within her soul.
And with a wink, nod and sigh,
She boldly walks by.

The Climb

Now Lucky was a sorrel horse, he stood sixteen hands,
He was gentle with the kids and quietly he stands,
Chrissy was a young girl, small and full of pride,
She asked her Ma if she could take Lucky for a ride.
"If you can get on you can ride," was her Ma's reply.
Chrissy went to get Lucky and give it a try.
Now Ma had a friend come to visit, just for the day,
Who was shocked at her friend and her parenting way.
"That is mean and cruel of what you make her do,
She is only a small child and under three-foot too.
There is no way that little girl can get on that horse,
I have a book on parenting I will give you of course.
I would never ask my kids to attempt such a task
for I would just lift them on and they wouldn't have to ask."

So they sat on the porch and watched from a distance,
As Chrissy worked at getting on without any assistance.
First it was a bucket, still Lucky was too high,
Then a ladder apparently had caught Chrissy's eye.
Then it was a barrel rolled on its side.
Lucky waited patiently at the things that Chrissy tried.
Next to a pole fence is where Lucky took his place,
As Chrissy slipped on his back, satisfaction crossed her face.
Ma's friend was silent as she watched Chrissy sit with pride,
Ma took a sip of coffee, "Keep your book," she sighed.
"You know I could of lifted her on him and they would have been fine,
But it is not the being there that is important,
It is the learning how to climb."

Kathy Moss

LAURALEE NORTHCOTT

Winthrop, Washington

Loving life and enjoying every minute of it seems to be Lauralee Northcott's mission. She is a professional musician, songwriter, pine-needle basket weaver, retired teacher, and a recently retired wilderness guide and pack cook.

As the bass player for the Horse Crazy Cowgirl Band (named 2014's "Best of the Best" Harmony Group by the Western Music Association), Lauralee also sings lead and harmony vocals. The group has a loyal international audience. She's written many songs that reflect her love for her home, horses, and the high country.

Because Lauralee was a public schoolteacher for more than twenty-five years, she had plenty of free time in the summers to be a guide and pack cook to guests riding over the steep and scenic trails of the Pasayten Wilderness, which lies adjacent to the Methow Valley in central Washington, which she calls home with her husband, Clayton. She worked on horseback every summer from 1983 through 2014 for professional outfitting companies, often spending all summer in the high country. During these times, she lived each day mixing work with delight, a motto that Lauralee has kept within her heart each day of her life. She feels that "enjoying life is a full-time job and the best work you'll ever get!"

The People Who Follow the Spring

When the heat comes back into the sun and winter is losing its hold,
First flowers tell of stories yet untold.
First the sunflowers in the low country, the lupine follow the tide,
And each in its turn works its way up the mountainside.

Chorus:
And the people who follow the spring, love horsetails in the sky,
They ride or walk to find themselves way up high
The land of spring awaits, it lives on, mountains high, lives on mountains high

Each meadow comes alive, as color invades its soul,
This is hope that you can touch, it's hope that you can hold.
Let's talk all day in the saddle, or never say a word,
Let's listen with our hearts, hear the stories to be heard.

Chorus

Lauralee Northcott

Yuppie Packer

There was a young man who had visions and dreams,
and he saw his life among the mountains and streams,
And he wanted to make his livin' in the hills,
For he knew he could handle the wrecks and the spills.

For he loves those moonlight nights out in the cold,
With campfires that burn and stories of old.
He was a traditional man in the Western way,
But modern needs got in his way.

And he's a yuppie packer, can't leave his phone behind
He's a yuppie packer callin' from the peaks on the off-peak times
He has to find to the highest spot, and climb to the sun.
To get a clear connection on Cellular One.

He knows that business and romance are uncomfortable mates,
So he acts ignorant of software and long distance rates.
He sneaks out of camp, as quiet as a mouse,
And nobody knows he has called down to the house.
He reminds his wife who he is, hears all the latest news
She recites his messages, he figures out all the business he will lose
And he muses how a laptop in his saddlebags might make life easier
And he wonders if the information superhighway is the sickness or the cure

Yeah, he's a yuppie packer and he really is cool,
He's a yuppie packer, heck he's even been to school.
He's got a Visa card, a MasterCard, even got an Eddie Bauer credit line
And he might even buy that stuff, if he only had the time.

She Speaks to Me

Sometimes he thinks about taxes as he's lookin' at the view
Mr. Audit dogs his tracks as he spits another chew
For how do you tell someone from Ogden, Utah,
That last hunting season was the last cash that you saw?
But tonight will find him listening for bells and snuggled up tight
He hopes those horses don't take it in their heads to travel tonight
He's livin' on the edge, but he likes the company,
Yet he kinda thinks: "This Western education might be killing me!"

Yeah, he's a yuppie packer, not gonna work harder, he's gonna work smart
If he can only convince seven mules, every one an orn'ry old fart.
So wish him the best, and hope his batteries will last,
'Til he passes that last crest, on Robinson Pass.

Lauralee Northcott

It's a Long Way from His Heart

Riding down the trail, the pack string passed us by.
Got to watching tracks when blood I did spy
Got a little worried seeing gear dropped in the path.
Rubber boots, lantern fuel, looked like the *Grapes of Wrath*
Turned out there'd been a great big wreck, cut up about three head.
When the packer started talkin', this is what he said:

Chorus:
Well, it's a long way from his heart, looks worse than it is.
When the bleeding stops we'll see just what he did
Yeah, it's a long way from his heart, so don't get too upset.
We've had some pretty bad tangles here, but we haven't lost one yet.

On a warm and sunny day, headed down the trail.
Everything was lovely 'til it started to derail.
A horse went over backwards, the rider hit a rock
And as her partner held her bleedin' head she asked her, "Can you talk?"
The packer tied up, checked her out and said she looks a sight.
Should be fine if you pull that hat down good and tight.

Chorus

There's been some awful spills and times that we've lived through.
Cross words have caused trouble a time or two.
 Sometimes the rope you've got just isn't long enough,
And when you come up short it can get pretty tough
Luckily, ineptitude and poor memory saves the day,
So when you see someone else's wreck this is what you'll say:

Chorus

We've had a few disasters here,
We've made a few mistakes that's clear, been cut ear to ear . . .
But we haven't lost one yet!

Lauralee Northcott

SKYE MESA OGILVIE

Missoula, Montana

Skye Mesa Ogilvie will go far as a poet and a songwriter. She grew up in a horse-trading and rodeoing family in Montana. She read Shakespeare and memorized poetry while riding colts out on the prairie. The high-headed broncs with faraway looks have taught her, hurt her, and healed her. Skye makes mohair tack, and rides over the ridges in South Dakota. She says, "I wrote this song a couple years ago for my sister and her husband. I hope you like it."

Cowgirl's Song
I know you're seeing the sunrise,
You're looking beyond these hills
Your cowboy heart is restless
But, oh my love, I love you still

You know I'm seeing the sunset
I'm looking beyond the hills
My cowgirl heart is restless
But, oh my love, you love me still

Your big grey is ready to go
But so is my bay, so is my bay

We're riding into the sunset
We're wandering across these hills
Our wild hearts are restless
But, oh my love, I love you still

Your big grey is rarin' to go
But, so is my bay, so is my bay
Together we'll ride to the sunset
A man, a grey, a girl, a bay

Skye Mesa Ogilvie

EVELYN ROPER

Gunnison, Colorado

Evelyn Roper, who lives in western Colorado, is a singer/songwriter, poet, painter, and photographer, as well as lead vocalist and rhythm guitarist for her band Opal Moon. She is a solo artist, half of the duo Original Recipe, and rhythm guitarist and vocalist for a new rockabilly band. Would you say she is a versatile talent? I certainly think so! Her style is Americana, reflected in Western swing, rockabilly, country, and the cowboy roots of Arizona, where she is from. Recording with other artists as harmony and lead vocals, several of her songs have also been chosen for released projects. Her song lyrics read like poetry, and I am glad to include her work here. I think she can best be described as "jalapenos and honey."

Opal Moon

Today's their anniversary, he'd promise to take her out
But cows don't care what day it is, that's what ranchin's all about
So, he's coming home late again, on this a special night
Figured he's in trouble again, so he braces for the fight
Yet when he steps through the doorway, full of sorry and regret
She meets him with a smiling face and not quite something he'd expect

She's turning off the TV and turns the radio on
After kicking off her shoes she leads him to the lawn
As the full moon comes up, she takes him by the hand
Snuggles close beside him and asks "May I have this dance?'"
He says "Darlin', I am sorry, I can't give you pretty things"
So in her softest voice, she begins to sing . . .

Jaded sagebrush, emerald hayfields in the summer
Amethysts and garnets of a western sunset sky
Golden aspen, satin evenings, in the autumn
Pearly snowflakes and the sapphires of your eyes

And today a turquoise morning and copper afternoon
Tonight, our love in the light of an Opal Moon

He draws her closer to him loving her with all his might
Tonight the gift she's given him assures him everything's alright
He knows she's always loved him, and forgives him for all his faults
As the cowboy and his woman dance a midnight, moonlit waltz
She says "By giving me your love, you give me everything"
And in her softest voice, she begins to sing . . .

Crystal raindrops, silvered lightning in the summer
Midnight diamonds on a black velvet sky
Ruby campfires, topaz hillsides, in the autumn
Platinum snow peaks and the sapphires of your eyes

And today a turquoise morning and a copper afternoon
Tonight, our love in the light of an Opal Moon

Precious moments, treasured memories with our children
The meadow perfume of a wildflower bouquet
Crazy laughter, time together when we find it
Your silken touches and honey kisses everyday

And today a turquoise morning and a copper afternoon
Tonight, our love in the light of an Opal Moon.

Evelyn Roper

SANDY SEATON SALLEE

Paradise Valley, Montana

Sandy Seaton Sallee rides and writes from her log cabin on the Yellowstone River in Paradise Valley, Montana. She and her husband, Scott, own and operate Black Mountain Outfitters, a horse and mule wilderness and ranch fishing and hunting camp. Sandy grew up driving four-up stagecoaches in Yellowstone National Park. She is a mountain horsewoman who loves to write poetry about the history of her area and her amazing experiences. She has been featured at the National Cowboy Poetry Gathering in Elko, Nevada, for many years, and performed at the first Montana Cowboy Poetry Gathering. Sandy writes articles for adventure magazines and is in demand as a lively emcee and entertainer.

The Price of the Pearl

Teenaged Mary shivered, pulled the threadbare blanket tight
The scratching of the branches woke her up again tonight
Huddled in her attic room, she cried a little prayer
Almighty God could see her soul and find a way to care.

A country girl, a workhorse, at ninety-seven pounds
To go to school, this brown-eyed girl was boarded out in town
Her landlord owned the Peale newsstand, livin' rich and high
And Mary's parents left her there to go to school and try

To help the woman mend her clothes and make her breakfast fare
Her son and nephew boarded and they needed Mary's care
She ironed all their silken shirts and kept their breakfast warm
The men would party wild at night and sleep late as the norm.

Pure white bedspreads sparkled, edged with shining lace
Except for little Mary, who had no sheets nor pillowcase
The dresser mirror broke in half, she sees her shadow pass
Hunched with fear and loneliness, a skinny sad young lass.

The house was very modern, had a tub and toilet, too
But Mary used a bucket and she made a spit bath do
She's a prisoner in the attic where rows of costumes swing
Milady danced in the Granada in a youthful fling.

Mary clutched her rosary and prayed deep in her heart
God would get her through this trial; He would take her part
1928, the times were tough for everyone
Mary dreamed of riding her mare Bess and having fun.

Mary watched the grandma who needed special care
When she shouted "little brown jug" in her crazed despair
Mary soothed the woman and tried to feed her meals
She wondered how she would survive her school year at the Peales.

The grandma had a parrot who roamed the house at will
So Mary cleaned the parrot's mess from floor and windowsill
The bird screeched "Woodrow Wilson" as he flew his rounds
Mary wished that she could fly and close out all the sounds.

The massive home had a gleaming rail of fancy plates
Mary dusted finery and cleaned the fireplace grates
She lugged the big coal buckets full of ashes out the door
Then started fresh new fires and kindled coal to roar.

Mary cleaned the vegetables, cooked the evening meal
The family dined by candlelight, but Mary knew the deal
Alone there in the kitchen, she had no supper choices
She ate in quiet loneliness and listened for their voices.

The woman had a lovely car, her son and nephew, too
Mary walked two miles to school when her chores were through
She'd stare back at the soulless house that held her future fast
Then wrapped her homemade coat against the winter's icy blast.

The Good Lord put her through the fire, the price, though of the pearl
She learned her grammar and her sums, this knowledge-hungry girl
The day her mother's horse and buggy pulled into the yard
Mary sobbed to point of breaking, said, "Mother, it's too hard

"To be treated as a servant without respect or pride."
Something in the tiny teen had shriveled up and died
Mrs. Peale offered five dollar bills to Mary's mother
But Mary ended school that day and never went another.

Mary never got an education, 'cept maybe how to care
She galloped 'round the farmstead on her speedy buckskin mare
This woman that's my grandma had no high school graduation
But she's a brilliant woman with a master's education!

Be Still. Let the Horse—Be a Horse

Don't push him to canter and lope figure eights
Don't prod him to side pass and open the gates
Don't pen him up lonely away from his mates
Don't hold him up tight just to see how he rates

Don't flag him and chase him and play with his mind
Don't scold him because he's sulled up in a bind
Don't watch him cross over, he can't move his hind
Don't cinch him unknowing, he's wearing a blind.

Don't spur him to sidepass and quicken his feet
Don't bribe him and stall him with many a treat
Don't bute him or ace him to make him compete
Don't make him the reason that your life's complete.

Be Still. Let the horse—be a horse.

'Cause sometimes a hoss must be wild and free
Unfettered, untouched, with complete liberty
To run if he wants to and buck and to flee
To be left alone—from you and from me.

A wet saddle blanket's helped many a steed
The right kind of training is sure what they need
But sometimes—just sometimes—step away from your lead
Let nature take over, renewing the breed.

Be Still. Let the horse—be a horse.

Sandy Seaton Sallee

We turn out our horses and mules every night
In one million acres, I sure love the sight
They're packing only a bell in their flight
Wrangled next morning, their eyes sparkle bright

A horse is as good as his breeding and care
They're willing to please, if you're kind and you're fair
But sometimes just leave them—stud, gelding, or mare
Ask them for nothing. Answer their prayer.

Be Still. Let the horse—be a horse.

Wolf

Silhouette drifts softly past my fire
Silence, then the pad of hardened feet
Slipping through the dark, becoming shyer
Time of birthing pups is near complete.
Black wolf, bad wolf, wolf within my dreams
Denning by the beaver dam below
Killed a bull elk, here to stay it seems
Drifting by me like an ancient flow.
Long-eared mules are stamping all around
Horses on their pickets rustle rope
Somewhere there! I hear a startled sound
She-wolf has departed at a lope.
I have dogs to guard me in the wild
Love them and they love me to a fault
Black wolf keeps them nervous and they're riled
Keep them chained in camp like it's a vault.
Mules, the Airedales, all our horses bright
Raised from babies, oh our lives entwined
She-wolf is an aching chilling sight
Mother and harbinger of her kind.
Tearing at her prey, their hearts still beating
Playing with their meat like it's a bone
Gorgeous wolf please be merely fleeting
Don't kill what I love and call my own.
Shadow wolf is howling like a child—My gun hand trembles . . . but I'm torn
My heart split by wolf and living wild—It's done . . . the wolf pups have been born.

ANN SOCHAT

Canutillo, Texas

"A storyteller in rhyme," is the way Ann Sochat describes herself. She has won the Will Rogers Award as Best Female Cowboy Poetry Performer from the Academy of Western Artists (AWA). She hails from Canutillo, Texas, and served as president of the Texas Cowboy Poets Association for three years. She has been a featured performer at cowboy symposiums and gatherings throughout the West.

The granddaughter of a cowboy and ranch foreman, Ann's love for the cowboy traditions is evident in her writing, as well as in her respect for the men and women who settled the West and are still found ranching it today.

Her poetry book, *Cowhide 'n Calico*, won the AWA Outstanding Poetry Book Award. Known for her entertaining style of delivery, Ann's poetry has been published in numerous magazines and anthologies.

Coffee's On

"Coffee's on. Come on in," my grandma used to say.
It was her standard greeting to all who passed her way.
She'd flash that great big smile, the screen door open wide,
And waving with her free hand, she'd usher them inside.
She had a lovely parlor, which she'd furnished with great care,
But it was in her kitchen where she'd sit them in a chair
Pulled up around her table, planks made of hand-hewn pine,
Worn smooth by generations as they gathered throughout time.
She always had some coffee, freshly brewed and hot;
She'd pour out steaming mugs from her old enameled pot.
And sitting 'round her table, folks would talk about their day:
About the weather, crops, and cattle, price of bales of hay,
Of children born and old friends gone, of holidays and kin,
Looking forward to tomorrow, reflecting on where they'd been.
Comforting the grieving, sharing someone's joy,
Offering advice to a lovesick young cowboy.
She always had some fresh bread. She really loved to bake.
She'd serve big slabs with butter, wrap some for you to take.
She'd drop a little morsel for the dog upon the floor
And shoo away the chickens from outside the kitchen door.
She made all people welcome; you were instantly aware
It wasn't just an act; she did genuinely care.
It's what everyone remembers and most missed when she was gone:
The legacy she left to me: "Come on in! Coffee's on!"

Ann Sochat

Diamonds

When they met, they were just teenage kids with dreams inside their heads;
He was a young cowboy, working on her father's spread.
Their courtship was a simple one as it began its course:
She would take him fresh-baked cookies; he would saddle up her horse.
He would help her as she gathered eggs from the chicken coop;
They would sit out talking in the evenings on the front porch stoop.
By the time her parents noticed it, there was nothing they could say.
The boy's manners were impeccable; he worked hard every day;
He did what he was supposed to, with nary a mistake.
Her father sighed as he admitted, "The boy's got what it takes!"
Still when the two came to them, her parents weren't prepared.
"Papa, we're in love!" she said. The boy stood, looking scared.
"Love!" her father agonized, as his wife burst into tears,
"You can't live on love! You're still wet behind the ears!"
But the young cowboy drew up straight. "Sir, I promise you,
I always will take care of her. I always will be true.
I know I don't have much right now; I haven't lots to give,
But I'll give her all the love I've got as long as we both live.
I'll work real hard; I plan to save; I've got the strength and nerve.
It won't be long, I'll give her all the things she does deserve."

And so the two were married in the little church in town.
He wore a slightly outgrown suit; she wore a plain white gown.
The wedding ring he gave her was a simple golden band,
But he whispered to her softly as he placed it on her hand.
"It isn't very fancy; 'twas the best that I could do,
But someday I'll buy you diamonds, dear. This I promise you."

Her folks fixed up the old foreman's place, and the kids soon settled in.
The two of them were as happy as they had ever been.
She planted a little garden; she cooked, she washed, she sewed.
They saved most all his salary; there was not a cent they owed.
He would talk to her in the evening of the things he planned to do.
"I'll get us land, a house, and cattle, and some diamonds, dear, for you."

The land came first, and then the house, though he still worked as a hand.
"Just one more year and we'll get some stock." And she seemed to understand.
But the next year brought a baby, and there were bills to pay.
And the next year, their well went dry, and they found, to their dismay
That they really needed two vehicles, so they had to buy a truck,
But Billy still would say to her, "We're having some bad luck,
But it will turn around. You'll see, within a year or two,
We'll have that herd of cattle, and some diamonds, dear, for you."
And she would always answer, "I wish I could make you see,
Though the diamonds mean a lot to you, they don't mean much to me.
I have you and have our little son and a roof over our head,
And one day soon we'll have fine cattle grazing on our spread."

Some more years passed, and they scrimped and saved. They were happy as can be.
When the phone rang on the afternoon of their anniversary,
It was Billy saying, "Listen. Here's what I want you to do.
I want you sitting on our porch this afternoon at two."
She hung the phone up, wondering, "What did that man devise?
I hope he hasn't spent our money on diamonds as a surprise!"
But she brushed her hair and changed her dress and looking at the clock,
She and her son went to the porch to sit and watch and rock.

Fifteen minutes passed and nothing; all she could do was trust,
And then in the distance, she saw a cloud of dust.
The dust cloud was drawing nearer; she stood so she could see.
Her heart beat fast; her mind was filled with incredulity.
Some shapes emerged, and she saw her father helping to guide their way,
Her brother was there and Billy too, riding on his big bay.
They drove the cattle past her as Billy came to a stop.
He wore a grin like a kid with money inside a candy shop.
He dismounted and came toward her, holding out his hand.
It was then that she looked and noticed the distinctive cattle brand.
She was seeing Billy's big surprise; into her mind it sank
As she watched a heifer run by, diamonds branded on its flank.
"A promise made is a promise kept; I wish it could be more,
You're the best wife that a man can have; remember when I swore
That I would give you diamonds? Well, those diamonds just walked by."
Then they laughed and kissed and hugged their son, and a tear did fill her eye.

There's a part of us that's sentimental. There is no use pretending
That all of us don't like a love story with a happy ending.
And perhaps we need reminding that some things in life come hard
But the road is made much easier when you have a loving pard.
So remember, that which is most valuable isn't always that which glitters.
Love your family, your land, your home, and respect all of God's critters.
Those two young people worked at it and found it to be true.
With faith and work, the diamonds that you seek will come to you.

An' How I'd Ride

I never will forget
The very first time that I saw it,
There I was a-walkin' down the street.
We had come in to the general store
To pick a few things up,
An' Pa gave me a nickel to buy some sweets.
As I moseyed to the ice cream parlor
To buy some penny candy,
Somethin' in Joe's window caught my eye,
The prettiest saddle I'd ever seen
Was sittin' on a stand,
I can't describe its beauty, but I'll try:
It was smooth an' shiny-lookin',
Not too fancy nor too plain,
With a little leather toolin' on back an' side,
An' I knew that if I just
Could put that saddle on my horse,
Gosh, Almighty, I would have the finest ride!

An' I'd ride out on the desert,
Out amongst the sage an' brush,
An' I'd feel the joy of bein' young an' free,
An' I'd chase them ole jackrabbits
'Roun' the sand hills with mesquite,
An' I would be so happy to be me!
—An' how I'd ride!

When I went into the store
Just so's I could touch the saddle,
There was lovin' admiration in my eyes!
An' Mrs. Joe, she came right up and said,
"Why don't you try it?
I do believe it's just about your size!"
An' my, but it felt fine
When I climbed into that seat.
I said, "Thank you kindly, Ma'am, for lettin' me try it.
I hope that saddle doesn't sell,
Cause I'm gonna save my nickels
An' when I've got enough, I'll come an' buy it!"

Ann Sochat

RHONDA STEARNS

Newcastle, Wyoming

Rhonda Stearns says she is proud to be a third-generation Wyoming rancher. Rhonda has spent most of six decades with cattle and horses. Reared within thirty miles of where both her grandfathers pioneered in the livestock business, she's followed many of their pony tracks.

Ranching, rodeoing, breeding, breaking, training, showing, and competing on horses have been her first loves. A national champion in high school rodeo, she moved on through successful years in amateur rodeo to the professional ranks, and is a Gold Card member of the Professional Rodeo Cowboys Association. The former Miss Rodeo Wyoming and National High School Rodeo Queen was inducted as a 1977 Cowgirl Honoree to the National Cowgirl Hall of Fame at Fort Worth, Texas.

As a cowboy poet she has been featured since the 1980s at many cowboy poetry gatherings in Wyoming, Montana, Idaho, North and South Dakota, Arizona, New Mexico, and Texas. In 2000 she became the first woman to receive the All-Around Cowboy Culture Award at the National Cowboy Symposium & Celebration at Lubbock, Texas. In 2003, the Academy of Western Artists named her Top Cowgirl Poet of the year.

Born to Ride*

"I was born to ride," this cowgirl says,
(She started when she was three!)
Horses have carried her through the years,
Brought her fame, and sights to see.

It began on her parents' homestead
On the wide Dakota plains,
But she has seen a lot of the world
Since she first picked up the reins.

Melvin Tivis (her cousin, you know),
Started her riding broncs.
This Meade County girl, not quite fifteen,
Found rodeo quite a romp!

Once in the saddle, she knew no fear,
But she wanted glamour, too—
Determined to learn trick-riding skills,
Many stunts she learned to do.

Seeking nothing less than perfection
She studied with Leonard Stroud;
Colorful, daring and fearless, she
Never failed to thrill the crowd!

Oklahoma Curly Roberts said,
"Speed up and do tricks faster."
Mattie took this advice to heart
And soon no one surpassed her.

They called her "The fastest trick rider
On the fastest horse around!"
With Frazier saddle and leather skirt
She thrilled fans in many towns.

Towns in Illinois, Indiana,
Kentucky and Iowa, too;
In Minnesota and Wisconsin,
She toured with Gardner's troupe.

Mattie rode quadrille, and Roman-raced,
And the relays she could win—
Sometimes leaping from horse to horse, a
Feat that would make your head spin!

She was stranded in Kentucky
When the show went belly-up;
But with cowgirl ingenuity
She got home—and thanked her luck!

Mattie rode for President Coolidge
At the Black Hills Roundup show.
Called to the stands to visit with him,
She found him quiet—nice to know.

Mattie's horses—Bob, Pal and Buster—
Were the pride of her young life.
She knew if you wanted a good horse
You must feed and "treat him right."

Rhonda Stearns

In the winter of 'Twenty-seven
Mattie became a wife.
She married rancher Maynard Newcombe
An' left the rodeo life.

For some sixty years they worked the ranch
Building it with hard labor.
Through Depression, drought and good times, too,
The Newcombes were good neighbors.

Mattie was injured by angry bulls,
But cowgirl grit pulled her through.
She lay, unconscious, eleven days,
Yet came out near good as new.

Mattie and Sissy were left alone—
Maynard crossed the Great Divide—
She's carried on as she knew he'd want,
Relyin' on cowgirl pride.

She's South Dakota's "Cowgirl Sweetheart,"
Named to many Halls of Fame;
She still loves glamour an' cowboy clothes—
Born to Ride—Mattie Goff, that's her name!

Written in honor of National Cowgirl Hall of Fame Honoree Mattie Goff Newcombe   —*Rhonda Stearns*

Full Circle

Whoa . . . easy son . . . after all, it's just a shadow;
Guess you were raised with dams an' cricks—never saw a windmill before.
Stand still son, an' I'll tell you, things that you should know . . .
That's it, take a drink from the tank, while I talk of the circle's lore.

Ancients deified it . . . Stonehenge . . . Medicine Wheel . . .
An' taught about the "Circle of Life" as a thing that had no end.
My wedding ring reminds me of that sacred deal;
Symbolically sealing, for eternity, man to mate and friend.

The season's circle 'crost the earth in that same way,
Seedtime an' harvest, sunshine an' rain, just the way it was ordained.
The sun an' moon, on their circles, make night and day,
An' sometimes real bad droughts take their toll . . . like the time it never rained.

Then we've got the bovine—the circle's in his blood—
As you learn to outfigure the cow, you'll find that I speak the truth . . .
You either break their circle, or you have a flood
Of hairy wild-eyed critters that'll turn you old amid your youth.

Even when they're in the "tub," in the workin' pens
They bunch, drop their heads, close their eyes an' circle, 'til you break them loose;
So doin', they try our patience—horses' and men's . . .
Confirmin' what we already knew—they've no more sense than a goose!

You an' me, son, we're two cogs in the wheel of life
Upon these plains, where the cowman has toiled a century and more . . .
Livin' thru pain . . . an' pleasure . . . an' plenty of strife . . .
Determined to hang onto the lifestyle by which he sets such store.

An' your fearsome windmill, that whirs an' squeaks an' pumps,
Provides the very lifeblood for you an' me . . . an' some stubborn cow.
An' this movin' circle, that gives your heart big thumps
Is nothin' but a shadow . . . or is it a prophecy somehow?

Could it mean our circle has just about played out?
That modern ways will kill us off, like dinosaurs an' unicorns?
Heck, son . . . there's work to do, let's leave here with a shout . . .
If our time's near, then we'll stampede . . . circled, right behind the longhorns.

She Speaks to Me

Fiddleback Headquarters

Step lightly, this is holy ground . . . made so by those who've gone before . . .
Don't you feel their aura, when you step in through that door?
Can't you sense their kinship? Feel their appraisal, and know that they're here?
Why would you laugh? Or act like they are somethin' to fear?

This Fiddleback Ranch home was built more than a hundred years ago,
Back in the eighteen-eightys, when life was hard . . . an' "slow" . . .
By that word I speak of how long it took to get a day's work done;
An' the way they always "found" a little time for fun.

Thousands of head of cattle, along with ten-thousands more of sheep
Wore the brand "Fiddleback"; an' their hands were short on sleep.
My husband's godmother cooked here, while her husband was the top hand
Who snapped out the Fiddleback rough string; all for the brand.

My mom's dad was a camp tender, drivin' miles of Fiddleback trail,
Packin' supplies to scattered herders, he could not fail.
Neither balky mules nor runaway teams deterred him from his chore . . .
Ridin' each ridge an' crick today, I recalled his lore.

I wonder . . . did he take off his hat, an' step 'crost this same threshold?
Look forward to the meal served up . . . taste the water cold . . .
Or did he maybe pump it, out there, where this bucket I just filled?
Did any hand who'd set at this table, in a horse wreck get killed?

Did they respect the quicksand? An' the sinkholes, the way we do?
Dread badger holes . . . slipp'ry banks . . . an' snakes that rattle, too?
Don'cha think they cursed the bovines, so danged determined to run free?
Didn't they fight heat an' drought.. . . an' the wind . . . constantly?

Rhonda Stearns

Betcha countless numb ol' fingers . . . an' frosted toes that burnt like sin . . .
Bunched, like us, 'round this ol' woodstove . . . thankful to be in,
From gatherin' an' movin' cows . . . that snow an' wind in their faces . . .
Glad like us to edge in . . . At table, take their places . . .

Reckon they've raced along the river, with the lightning crackin' wild?
Then, when they'd turned the bunch, were they happy as a child?
Did they fight their broncs to face that wind, when small hail come stingin' down?
Ride like hell to some cut bank . . . 'fore the big stuff did pound?

Did they know the blessed comfort, to stretch out upon the warm sand . . .
Rare respite from constant tension, ridin' for the brand?
Did they give their all to stick some bronc, while dodgin' cottonwood limbs?
Don't it kinda cross over . . . their world, an' ours, my friends?

Haven't their horses jolted them, jumpin' over a white-tailed fawn . . .
All bedded down an' hidin', just before break of dawn?
Did they love to hear elk bugle, as the sun sank beyond the rim,
That bordered their world? Did they think of God . . . and thank Him?

Sci-fi folk talk of "time warp" . . . an' sometimes I'm sure I have been there . . .
When sittin' around this table . . . eatin' cowboy fare . . .
Reckon I've earned their approval? That would be the greatest of all
Honors, awards or trophies, given by some famed Hall . . .

Each time I ride for the Fiddleback, I hope to please these "old ones" . . .
Unworthy though I am . . . alongside of such bold ones.
What a priv'lege . . . to step inside this door, an' tread their holy ground . . .
Please . . . let 'em sense my rev'rence, Lord . . . as they gather 'round . . .

JODY STRAND

Baker, Montana

Rhonda Stearns, one of the poets in this book, directed me to this poet. She said, "Jody Strand is a hardworking wife, mother, and a good neighbor. She always wanted to be a cowboy. Marrying a cowboy turned her into a hired hand, and she spent a lot of her life working on ranches and cowboying in several states."

When I asked Jody to tell me about herself, she wrote, "It's hard to write your own bio, ya know? I was raised on a farm in Minnesota but from my earliest childhood I always wanted a horse and to be a cowboy." It only seemed natural that she would marry a ranch hand and live on the ranches where her husband worked. "Many times I was his only help, so through his teaching, and trial and error, I learned to be that cowboy I'd dreamed about," she said. "I'd just never known way back when how much work being a cowboy was!"

From that rich background of experience, Jody began writing and performing fine cowboy poetry at many venues across the West, starting in the early 1980s. Most recently she served as director of a small town museum. She's now keeping a big yard and garden—while claiming she's "enjoying retirement." The job she loved the best, she told me, was ranch work. "I loved the horses and the good people I met along the way. In my heart I'll always be a cowboy."

The Hired Man

My son came home from school one day
and he had a big black eye
I asked him how he got it
and this was his reply

He said, "Mom some kids made fun of me
they said dad's just a hired man
we don't own our own house or cattle
we don't even own any land

They say that we're just drifters
we can't keep a job for long
that I'll never amount to nothin'
and we'll just keep movin' on

I told him, "Son that's just not true
those kids don't understand
how many special things it takes
to be a hired man

Your daddy's not a drifter
He'd love to settle down
to find a better place for us
is why he moves around

A nicer house, a higher wage
a better school for you
that's why all kinds of people move
to better their lives too

Your daddy'd love to have a ranch
to call his own some day
but there was no ranch to hand down
so he has to work for pay

Your dad could go to work in town
and wear a suit and tie
but that's not who or what he is
and here's the reason why

If there were no more hired men
big ranches would be gone
one man can't do it all alone
even working from dusk 'til dawn

Large herds of cattle would be no more
Just bunches here and there
the stores piled high with beef today
would someday soon be bare

Farmers would have to cut down too
land would just lay idle
breadbasket of the nation
would no longer be our title

Hired man, why they're just words
but they should be said with pride
for they're agriculture's backbone
without them it would have died

And as to what your future holds
well Son, that's up to you
but take a lesson from your dad
be proud of what you do.

The Hired Man's Wife

With the job the housing's furnished
but the house is not your own
and every time you have to move
you grumble and you groan

You just got to know the neighbors
and your bedroom curtains came
your seeds just came up in the garden
and the preacher can call you by name

You finally got the house fixed up
the leaky faucets and busted screens
you've shampooed the rugs and washed the walls
and scrubbed and shined and cleaned

You trimmed the trees and mowed the yard
and you've got some flowers growing
but now that you've made this place your home
You'll be leaving soon you're knowing

'cause once you get all settled in
and start planning for next year
You know that he'll come in one day
and say, "You better start packing dear

"I heard about a better job
where we could run cows of our own
the pay is good and the housing's furnished
so pack up and let's get goin'"

You take down all the pictures
pack your dishes and your clothes
walk through your half-grown garden
wipe your tears and blow your nose

He's trying to make life better
trying hard to get ahead
and he will never understand
the lonely tears you shed

That housing that was furnished
was like unmolded clay
you worked and shaped it into your home
and forgot you couldn't stay

Now it's time for you to move again
and reluctantly you'll go
but part of you will stay behind
to watch your garden grow

How can you start over again and again
some other women ask
we simply smile because we know
we're equal to the task

Ranch hands' wives have a special gift
for accepting what we've been handed
and to live this cowboy life we love
we'll grow anywhere we're planted

Cowboy Pride

A housewife and a mother
were all she was it seemed
but she craved a different title
in her heart and in her dreams

Whenever help was needed
She'd saddled up her horse
to move or sort or gather
and then nature took its course

She learned the ways of cattle
where to be and how they think
how to spot a cow that's calving
by her tail held in a kink

When it came to working cattle
she wanted to belong
but the men said they were working
and she was just along

She knew she'd filled the holes and gaps
as well as any man
and all she ever wanted
was to just be called a hand

But no one ever said it
and it hurt deep down inside
though she'd rather never hear it
than to know somehow they'd lied

The day was hot and humid
when the boss pulled up to say
two hundred pairs are leaving
cut 'em from the herd today

Jody Strand

153

The trucks would load at nightfall
to go to better grass
mistakes were not an option
each cow must have her calf

At dinner they suggested
she could maybe watch a gate
and they just might get done faster
so it wouldn't get so late

She stacked up all the dishes
grabbed her boots and hat and then
she caught her horse and saddled up
and rode out with the men

She did her share of sorting
peeling back pair after pair
then she took her turn up by the gate
and did a good job there

The day stretched on and still they worked
but she was glad inside
for the chance to be there with them
to work cattle and to ride

She spilled a calf and had to race
to head it from the herd
full speed through mud and cut banks
but she never said a word

When day was done and supper ate
the men talked and she listened
recounting what they'd done that day
while she cleaned up the kitchen

and then her name was mentioned
and a story they did tell
of her silent race to catch that calf
and how she'd done it well

"We'd a'helped her if she'd hollered
our backs was to her ride
but she never yelled to us for help
now that's pure dumb cowboy pride."

She was stiff and sore and tired
but her heart had just took flight
'cause without their even knowin' it
she got her due that night

A hand they hadn't called her
but now she was one of them
'cause cowboy pride had always been
reserved for just the men.

TINA WILLIS

Wheatland, Wyoming

Trina Campbell was very firm when she said, "When I was asked who my favorite cowgirl poet was, I had no doubt in my mind the artist I wanted to see in this anthology was Tina Willis! Her poetry is wonderful!"

Tina, born on a remote Wyoming ranch sixty miles southwest of Casper on the North Platte River, began writing poetry when she was a little girl. She spent many years working with cows and sheep on several Wyoming ranches, becoming very proficient at herding bulls and roping steers. "I have spent my lifetime learning that being a cowboy is a job . . . not a gender," she says. "I believe cowboy poetry is a folk art born in the shadows and flames of flickering campfires. This art is rekindled each time cowboys gather to remember the old stories and poems."

Tina was one of the first women to appear on the night show at the National Cowboy Poetry Gathering in Elko, Nevada, in 1986, and she has represented Wyoming on five different occasions at the national gathering. She has appeared thirteen times at the Wyoming Cowboy Poetry Roundup and has performed throughout West.

She is the recipient of the Neltje Blanchan Award, presented for outstanding creative writing from the Wyoming Arts Council. She says about her life as a poet, "I have performed several hundred times over the past nearly thirty years. I have shared my poetry while standing on grand stages with thousands of people in attendance, but I have been just as proud reading it around a campfire for tired cowboys."

With His Face to the Wind

He speaks true words and he means them; he stands out among honorable men
As he clings to his last shreds of freedom, he rides out with his face to the wind

He measures each man by his handshake; doesn't care for money or wealth
He won't admit he ever was lonely on those nights he spent alone with himself

He is glad to share coffee and campfire; and he has no fear of death . . . just respect
If he loses a stirrup at daybreak, well heck it was only a little wreck

He lives in the days of his grandfather; wishing time would only stand still
Knowing his fight against progress is futile; it's like pushing his rope up a hill

He may share his dreams and his longings if he can put the words in a song
And he may give her a glimpse of his loving, should the right woman dare come along

He drinks whiskey that crossed Canada's border 'til he remembers the steps to the dance
He will be horseback until his last moments, if God will just give him the chance

He'll rise to see sun up each morning; to ride out with other good men
And the most he will ask from his Maker, is a ride home with his back to the wind

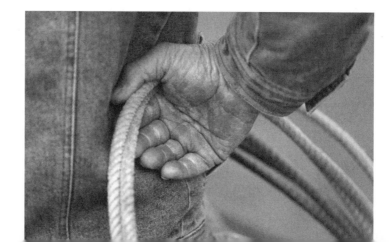

A Cowboy Defends Us

I wonder what it means to you
When you see the flutter of red, white and blue
I think of American history and days that are gone
I think of our troops in Iraq and Iran

I think of the folks that settled this West
Who raised sons and daughters and offered their best
Their children traded a tractor for a Humvee rough ride
Their parents now wait with no sleep but with pride

I think of the cowboy called to duty today
Throwing his pony a last flake of hay
Before boarding a bus in this dawn's early light
As he joins the forces to fight the good fight

I think of the bunkhouse with one empty bed
There's a tent in the sand where he now lays his head
As I savor my freedom and pray for our troops
There is a cowboy now wearing infantry boots

His instincts and courage were learned on the range
He's taking care of the homestead with a scenery change
Our nation is safer and stronger today
Because a cowboy defends us . . . time zones away

And I wonder what it means to you
When you see the flutter of red, white and blue . . .

Tina Willis

157

Side by Side

We welcomed the storm as a sure sign of spring; green hills follow a late April snow
But death came on the wind as it howled from the north; the worst blizzard I'll ever know
For three days the cows fought against it, until the hair had been beat from their hide
Backs humped up and covered with ice, they suffered there, side by side

They stood with their backs against the barrage; protecting their young as best as they could
The rain turned to snow; then the snow into drifts; the calves began to drop where they stood
The fence held the cows for the first couple days, as the storm came in waves like the tide
By then the lead had been pushed to the ground, and they perished there, side by side

The cows moved out from in front of the wind; blindly they fought from the blast
Each fence line and cut back for miles and miles claimed the ones that gave up at last
When the storm finally broke, we followed their tracks, for a ten-mile stretch, and I cried
Back down that trail, we brought them home . . . a few cows . . . a few calves, side by side

We spent long hours horseback and many on foot, looking for just one more calf left alive
The loss was shared by our neighbors and friends; how we prayed that we all would survive
Calves lost their mommas and mommas their calves; together we tried to pair up a few
But some cows wouldn't claim their very own calf, and the next cow would leave, taking two
The twenty-hour days all ran together; I tried to forget the good cows that died
I walked miles with God, with my dog at my heels; we'd collapse each night side by side

Now the hills did become green, and spring did return; the pain and snow melted away
We mixed milk for bum calves in a five-gallon jug and I found more faith every day
The need to hold on, to go on, to just live, became part of my summer routine
And I was reminded one more time of this, that fall when it came time to wean
One old black cow with a lump on her jaw knew what it took to survive
She nuzzled her calf and an orphan she'd claimed, as they nursed her side by side

THANKS AND GRATITUDE

"Poetry is plucking at the heartstrings, and making music with them."

—D. Gabor

To Erin Turner, who has been my editor at Two Dot for all my books, and is always encouraging.

To Jennifer Denison for believing in this book and for graciously writing the foreword.

To Robin L. Green, who is my dear friend as well as a great photographer, whose images were all handpicked for these poems and songs.

To Michael Everson, my Top Hand, for, again, keeping my ropes untangled, my fences tight, and for bringing the book to the shipping point.

To Jessica Hedges, who pointed me in a direction to gather.

To all the poets and songwriters who shared their work so graciously, so that your heartstrings would be plucked as mine were.

—Jill Charlotte Stanford

SOURCES

The first place you will want to go after reading through this book is the website for Western and Cowboy Poetry, Music & More at the Bar-D Ranch, "preserving and celebrating the arts and life of rural communities and the real working West," at www .cowboypoetry.com. Nearly all the poets in this book are waiting to meet you there. Music, history, books, and CDs make this the most comprehensive site furthering cowboy and cowgirl poetry and music.

AUKER, Amy Hale, pages 1–7
Amy Hale Auker is online at www.amyhaleauker.com, www.cowboypoetry.com, and on Facebook, Instagram, and Twitter. Some information in her bio is provided courtesy of www.amyhaleauker.com.

BATES, Sally, pages 8–14
Find more of this Arizona cowgirl poet's work at www.cowboypoetry.com/sallyharperbates.htm.

BENNETT, Virginia, pages 15–22
Now my dear friend—and I stand in complete awe of her—Virginia Bennett has a wonderful write up at www.cowboypoetry.com/vibennett.htm.

BERG, Niki, pages 23–25
Watch and listen to Niki at www.youtube.com/watch?v =X-JHd9cgSYc.

BURLESON, Teresa, pages 26–32
"Cowboy Poetry the Cowgirl Way" are almost the first words you see when you go to www.teresaburlcson cowgirlpoet.com. You get the added bonus of hearing her recite a poem, too. You can also find Teresa's poetry at Tammy Goldammer's always interesting, sometimes hair-raising, very funny and insightful blog about her life on her ranch with her faithful cow dogs. You can begin your day (or end your evening) with her too, here at www.tammys cowdogs.com.

DALEY, Doris, pages 33–37
Way up in Alberta, Canada, Doris Daley writes a blog. To read this, as well as for information about upcoming events where she will be reading her poetry, find her at www. dorisdaley.com.

GILBERTSON, Janice, pages 38–42
A lovely place to visit is Janice Gilbertson's website, http:// janicegilbertsonwriter.com/page-2 where she shares her poetry and her life.

HANKINS, Audrey, pages 43–46
This cowgirl poet says she was "raised on good grass." See for yourself at www.cowboypoetry.com/audreyhankins.htm.

HARMS, Joni, pages 47–48
You can find all the CDs of this delightful singing cowgirl at www.joniharms.com. Some information in her bio is provided courtesy of her website www.joniharms.com.

HASSELSTROM, Linda, pages 49–53
Visit www.windbreakhouse.com for nearly all the information you might want on Linda Hasselstrom. Her blog, at windbreakhouse.wordpress.com, is a joy to read. If you would like to attend one of her writing retreats, write to: Windbreak House Writing Retreats, PO Box 169, Hermosa, SD 57744; voicemail (605) 255-4064.

HEDGES, Jessica, pages 54–57
Poet, mother of two small boys, wife of Buckaroo Sam, and entrepreneur, Jessica has more to tell at www.jessicahedges cowboypoetry.com/home.

HILL, Debra Coppinger, pages 58–63
Debra Coppinger Hill loves to laugh and live life, and it shows on her homepage, www.alwayscowboy.net/debra_coppinger_hill_poetry.html. Some information in her bio is provided courtesy of her website.

HOLLENBECK, Yvonne, pages 64–69
Award-winning poet and quilter, Yvonne Hollenbeck's page, www.yvonnehollenbeck.com is lovely—like her poems!

JENNE, Stacy, pages 70–72

JOHNSON, Dee Strickland, pages 73–78
Dee Strickland Johnson, aka "Buckshot Dot," can be found on www.buckshotdot.com. A complete listing of her books and CDs is a treat! Some information in her bio is provided courtesy of her website.

JOHNSON, Randi, pages 79–84
This young, beautiful, and upcoming buckaroo poet can be seen reciting one of her poems at www.youtube.com/watch?v=LDXi3Tps-K8.

KIRKWOOD, Jo Lynne, pages 85–89
Jo Lynne Kirkwood's books and CDs are: *A Cowboy Season* (CD); *Old Stories* (a collection of poems); *A Cedar Ridge Christmas* (CD); *Somewhere in the West* (CD); and *Hay, Baby!* (CD). You can contact her at www.jokirkwood.com.

KLAPROTH, Echo, pages 92–95
Echo Klaproth can be viewed reciting a terrific poem at www.youtube.com/watch?v=iEePI-rHpp0. Part of her bio was provided courtesy of K-12 Wyoming Social Studies Teachers Summit Guide.

McCALL, Deanna Dickinson, pages 96–100
Deanna is the author of *Mustang Spring* by the Frontier Project; author and performer of *Riding*, a poetry CD; and author and performer of *Hot Iron*, a cowboy poetry CD. You will find her books and award-winning CD, plus a lot more, at www.deannadickinsonmccall.com, including information on her newly published book, *Rough Patches*. Some information in her bio is provided courtesy of her website.

MEADOR, Renee, pages 101–105
Renee's story and a few more poems can be found at www
.cowboypoetry.com/reneemeador.htm.

MESSERSMITH, Lyn, pages 106–110
Lyn does not have her own website but you can read more
about her as well as other poems at www.cowboypoetry
.com/lynmessersmith.com.

MOSS, Kathy, pages 111–115
The portal to this poet's books and upcoming events is
www.akmossbooks.com.

NORTHCOTT, Lauralee, pages 116–121
How can you *not* love someone who is in a band
called Horse Crazy Cowgirl Band (at www.
horsecrazycowgirlband.com). You can see her basket work
at the local gallery in Winthrop, Washington, or visit www
.winthropgallery.com.

OGILVIE, Skye Mesa, pages 122–123
Skye's website is www.cielocinches.com. Hand-tied,
100-percent mohair cinches and breast collars—comfort
for your horse and style for you!

ROPER, Evelyn, pages 124–125
You can sample some of this songwriter's music by going to
www.reverbnation.com/evelynroperopalmoon.

SALLEE, Sandy Seaton, pages 126–131
Hankering to get away from it all? Contact Sandy Seaton
Sallee at Black Mountain Outfitters, Inc./Slough Creek
Outfitters, PO Box 117, Emigrant, MT 59027; (406) 222-
7455; www.blackmountainoutfitters.com or www
.sloughcreekoutfitters.com.

SOCHAT, Ann, pages 132–139
You can read more about this winner of the Academy
of Western Artists' Will Rogers Award as Best Female
Cowboy Poetry Performer for 2000 at www.cowboypoetry.
com/annsochat.htm. Some information in her bio is
provided courtesy of cowboypoetry.com.

STEARNS, Rhonda, pages 140–147
Mosey on over to Rhonda's website and read about her life,
poetry, and books: www.doublespearranch.com/rhonda
-sedgwick-stearns.html. Some information in her bio is
provided courtesy of her website.

STRAND, Jody, pages 148–154
Jody Strand, a Montana cowgirl, has a lovely poem you can
read at www.cowboypoetry.com/jodystrand.htm.

WILLIS, Tina, pages 155–158
Calling herself a "cowboy poet," Tina Willis can be
contacted at PO Box 913, Wheatland, WY 82201.

ABOUT THE AUTHOR

Jill Charlotte Stanford considers herself the luckiest person in the world. Growing up admiring them from afar, from the fifth row of the darkened Princess Theater in Edmonds, Washington, malt balls slowly melting in her hot little fist, cowgirls like Dale Evans and others certainly shaped her dreams and her future. She never dreamed, then, that she would grow up and someday meet and write about real cowgirls. From her first book to this one, her circle has grown to include ranchers, trick riders, horse trainers, and breeders, and now, poets and songwriters that write of the West. They have all proven to be women of resourcefulness, courage, humility, great humor, and a generous spirit.

A little girl wearing small, red cowboy boots came up to Jill at a book signing not too long ago. Eying her fringed jacket and looking her square in the eye (in true cowgirl fashion), she asked, "Are you a *real* cowgirl?" Jill looked her back square in the eye and replied, "I sure hope so!" You can see all her books at www.jillcharlotte.com.

ABOUT THE PHOTOGRAPHER

Self-taught photographer Robin L. Green lives in Ellensburg, Washington, with her Jack Russell, Jasper, and her horse, The Bay Mare. Considering herself much more intuitive than technical, she is drawn to her subjects as more of a casual observer than choreographer. She makes her living photographing a wide range of people and animals, senior portraits, and unforgettable wedding albums. But Western backdrops are still, after many years, her favorite "subject" to shoot.

For Robin, photography is an expression of thought and an interpretation of what she sees: "It is a blessing and a gift to see light and composition in even the most ordinary situations, and capturing it is a way to hold onto it whereas we might not otherwise." You can find Robin's work on Facebook under Robin L Photography. Her website is www.thebaymare.com.